UNSOLVED
MYSTERIES

Publications International, Ltd.

Written by:
Patricia Barnes-Svarney, Fiona Broome, Robert Bullington, William W. David, Colleen Delegan, Tom DeMichael, Katherine Don, James Duplacey, Mary Fons, Linda Godfrey, John Gorenfeld, R.G.W. Griffin, Peter Haugen, Jonathan W. Jordan, J.K. Kelley, David Lesjak, Shanon Lyon, Bill Martin, Patricia Martinelli, Katherine McGowan, Mary Fons-Misetic, Paul Morie, Kimberly Morris, Richard Mueller, Peter Muggeridge, Eric D. Nelson, Robert Norris, Jay Rath, Russ Roberts, Lawrence Robinson, Allen Smith, Peter Suciu, Don Vaughan, Amanda Wegner, James Willis

Photography from Commons.wikimedia.org and Shutterstock.com

TABLE OF CONTENTS

INTRODUCTION

Some events are beyond explanation. Lacking any signs of provenance, they manifest themselves in ways that don't wholly make sense in our rational world of cause and effect. We use logic to try to understand this whirling mess of mass expanding infinitely beyond us, but we fall short of the task because the universe doesn't package itself as neatly as we might expect. But let alone the universe for now. We seemingly have a stronger grasp on more terrestrial affairs, but there is still much that happens on this earth that puzzles our empirical logic. Objects and people appear and disappear mysteriously, facts dissipate into the ether, rumors abound, and bygone traditions continue to be practiced while their true significances were lost long ago.

Life on earth comes in many shapes, and there is no doubt that we've only touched the tip of the iceberg when it comes to knowing all of its forms. Beasts lurk in the woods outside of the city, weary of the activities of humanity. Suspicions arise from mysterious deaths, and disappearances of people leave no clues to be followed. Their endings are never clarified, and we are left to live with the possibility of never really knowing the truth.

There are phenomena we will never understand, and experiences we believe we understand but do not. We have intuitions that prove to be true without knowing how or why. Not everything follows the rules of logic, and not everything can be deduced from cause and effect.

Cryptozoology, parapsychology, uncaught killers, paranormal activity, extraterrestrials, forgotten history, and all types of fringe science fill the pages of *Unsolved Mysteries,* leaving you with more questions than answers. When nothing seems to add up into a logical conclusion, intuition is far more reliable in these situations than the cold, hard rigor of the scientific method.

Use *Unsolved Mysteries* to open yourself up outside of the categories of civilization. Never think you know, and never think you don't know. Look for the answers but never claim the solution. Unsolved mysteries proliferate in your everyday experience. Can you look close enough to see them?

CHAPTER 1
MYSTERIOUS ORIGINS & ENDINGS

THE WORLD'S FIRST CIVILIZATION

The fame of the ancient Egyptians—pyramids, pharaohs, eye makeup!—has led to the common misconception that ancient Egypt was the world's first civilization.

Most Western scholars agree that the Sumerian civilization in Mesopotamia, located between the Tigris and Euphrates rivers in modern-day Iraq, was the first. Yet a deeper look reveals that there is a whole pageant of contenders for that coveted prize.

THE CONTESTANTS

1. Ancient Sumer: The first civilization is believed to have begun around 4000 BC. The great city of Ur, associated with Sumer, is possibly the world's first city. Archaeological evidence suggests that "pre-civilized" cultures lived in the Tigris and Euphrates river valleys long before the emergence of Sumer.

2. The Harappan: Next in line are the ancient Indus Valley civilizations, located in the Indus and Ghaggar-Hakra river valleys in modern-day Pakistan and western India. The first mature civilization associated with this area is called the Harappan, generally cited as beginning around 3500 BC, thus placing it in time after Sumer. However, it is clear that agricultural communities had inhabited the area since at least 9000 BC.

3. Ancient Egypt: Located in Africa's Nile Valley, it is generally cited as beginning in 3200 BC. But as with the Indus Valley civilization, it is difficult to establish a firm beginning date because agricultural societies had settled in the Nile River Valley since the 10th millennium BC.

4. Ancient China and Elam: The final two, and least known, contestants (from the Western perspective) are the ancient Chinese civilizations and the Elam civilization of modern-day Iran. The Elamite kingdom began around 2700 BC, though recent evidence suggests that a city existed in this area at a far earlier date—perhaps early enough to rival Sumer. Meanwhile, the ancient Chinese civilizations, located in the Yangtze and Yellow river valleys, are said to have begun around 2200 BC.

THE CRITERIA

The most salient feature of a civilization is a city, which, unlike a village, should have large religious and government buildings, evidence of social stratification (mansions for the rich and shacks for the poor), and complex infrastructure such as roads and irrigation. Civilizations are also defined by elaborate social systems, organized trade relations with outside groups, and the development of writing.

Marking a "civilization" is difficult because in all five possible cradles of civilization described above, complex societies lived in the same areas long before true civilization emerged. In fact, this is surely why civilizations first developed in these regions—human groups lived in the areas before the development of agriculture. Human populations have roamed the sprawling Eurasian continent for at least 100,000 years.

The emergence of civilization can be seen as the result of culture after culture living in one geographic area for countless generations until something happened that set these seminomadic groups on the path to civilization.

A DISCOVERY OF BIBLICAL PROPORTIONS

While rounding up a stray animal near Qumran, Israel, in early 1947, Bedouin shepherd Mohammed el-Hamed stumbled across several pottery jars containing scrolls written in Hebrew. It turned out to be the find of a lifetime.

News of the exciting discovery of ancient artifacts spurred archaeologists to scour the area of the original find for additional material. Over a period of nine years, the remains of approximately 900 documents were recovered from 11 caves near the ruins of Qumran, a plateau community on the northwest shore of the Dead Sea. The documents have come to be known as the Dead Sea Scrolls.

Tests indicate that all but one of the documents were created between the middle of the 2nd century BC and the 1st century AD. Nearly all were written in one of three Hebrew dialects. The majority of the documents were written on animal hide.

The scrolls represent the earliest surviving copies of Biblical documents. Approximately 30 percent of the material is from the Hebrew Bible. Every book of the Old Testament is represented with the exception of the Book of Esther and the Book of Nehemiah. Another 30 percent of the scrolls contain essays on subjects including blessings, war, community rule, and the membership requirements of a Jewish sect. About 25 percent of the material refers to Israelite religious texts not contained in the Hebrew Bible, while 15 percent of the data has yet to be identified.

Since their discovery, debate about the meaning of the scrolls has been intense. One widely held theory subscribes to the belief that the scrolls were created at the village of Qumran and then hidden by the inhabitants. According to this theory, a Jewish sect known as the Essenes wrote the scrolls. Those subscribing to this theory have concluded that the Essenes hid the scrolls in nearby caves during the Jewish Revolt in AD 66, shortly before they were massacred by Roman troops.

A second major theory, put forward by Norman Golb, Professor of Jewish History at the University of Chicago, speculates that the scrolls were originally housed in various Jerusalem-area libraries and were spirited out of the city when the Romans besieged the capital in AD 68–70. Golb believes that the treasures documented on the so-called Copper Scroll could only have been held in Jerusalem. Golb also alleges that the variety of conflicting ideas found in the scrolls indicates that the documents are facsimiles of literary texts.

The documents were catalogued according to which cave they were found in and have been categorized into Biblical and non-Biblical works. Of the eleven caves, numbers 1 and 11 yielded the most intact documents, while number 4 held the most material—an astounding 15,000 fragments representing 40 percent of the total material found. Multiple copies of the Hebrew Bible have been identified, including 19 copies of the Book of Isaiah, 30 copies of Psalms, and 25 copies of Deuteronomy. Also found were previously unknown psalms attributed to King David, and stories about Abraham and Noah.

Most of the fragments appeared in print between 1950 and 1965, with the exception of the material from Cave 4. Publication of the manuscripts was entrusted to an international group led by Father Roland de Vaux of the Dominican Order in Jerusalem.

Access to the material was governed by a "secrecy rule"—only members of the international team were allowed to see them. In late 1971, 17 documents were published, followed by the release of a complete set of images of all the Cave 4 material. The secrecy rule was eventually lifted, and copies of all documents were in print by 1995. Many of the documents are now housed in the Shrine of the Book, a wing of the Israel Museum located in Western Jerusalem. The scrolls on display are rotated every three to six months.

THE RELISHED RELIC

Relics are an important element in several of the world's major religions. These ancient holy artifacts—thought to be pieces of a saint's or a significant leader's body or one of their personal belongings—are said to be imbued with spiritual power and are highly protected. But are they real or not? As some believers would say, you just have to have faith. Many people dispute the authenticity of these holy objects. For example, it's impossible to be 100 percent sure that an old sword actually belonged to the real Saint Peter. Even so, people come from all over the world just to bask in the presence of these (often odd) artifacts.

THE HOLY PREPUCE

According to New Testament apocrypha (writings by early Christians about Jesus and his teachings that were not accepted into the holy canon), after baby Jesus was circumcised, an old Jewish woman saved his foreskin. But by the Middle Ages, several different foreskins were touted as the original and were worshipped as holy relics by various churches. Stories abound of various prepuces gifted to monks, stolen by thieves, dismissed by Popes, and marched in parades, all adding to the mystery of this particular relic.

THE TOOTH OF BUDDHA

After the Buddha died (approximately 500 BC), it's said that his body was cremated. As the story goes, after the cremation, a follower retrieved the Buddha's left canine tooth from the funeral pyre. The tooth was given to the king and quickly became legendary: Whoever claimed the tooth would rule the land. Wars were fought over possession of the tooth for centuries, and now the tooth—or what's left of it 2,500 years later—rests in a temple in Sri Lanka.

THE SACRED RELICS

From the 16th to 19th centuries, sultans of the Ottoman Empire collected religious items of the Islamic faith. Most were said to be relics of various Islamic prophets, though many of the pieces are of questionable origin. Included in the collection, now held in Istanbul, are Moses's staff, a pot belonging to Abraham, and a piece of the prophet Muhammad's tooth. Perhaps the most important of the relics is the Blessed Mantle, the black wool shawl said to have been placed on a poet's shoulders by Muhammad himself.

RELICS OF SAINTE-CHAPELLE

If you find yourself in Paris, visit Notre Dame to behold the collection of Sainte-Chapelle relics, including shards of the True Cross (believed to be actual wood from Christ's cross), relics of the Virgin Mary, the Mandylion (a piece of fabric similar to the Shroud of Turin on which Christ's face is said to appear), and something called the Holy Sponge, a blood-stained sponge that was said to be offered to Christ to drink from when he was languishing on the cross. The authenticity of these objects is as contested as any on this list, but the items are impressive if nothing else for surviving the French Revolution.

VERONICA'S VEIL

According to tradition, a woman named Veronica (she's not mentioned by name in the Bible) wiped the face of Jesus on his way toward Calvary. The fabric she used was said to have taken the imprint of Jesus' face. The veil can now be found in St. Peter's Basilica in Rome. Or maybe it's held in a friary outside of Rome—there's another version of the veil there. Regardless, plenty of people claim to have seen the bloodstained face of Jesus in the fabric of Veronica's veil and continue to make pilgrimages to worship it.

THE SHROUD OF TURIN

Of all the relics on this list, the Shroud of Turin is the one whose authenticity remains the most hotly debated, even more than 100 years after its discovery. Carbon dating originally proved the material, purportedly the shroud laid over Christ at the time of his burial, was produced in the Middle Ages, but it has since been proven incorrect—the garment is in fact older. Perhaps most fascinating about the Shroud is that the image itself is a negative; photographic methods were hardly known at the time of Christ's death, so how could anyone have faked such an image?

THE SHROUD OF TURIN: REAL OR FAKE?

Measuring roughly 14 feet long by 3 feet wide, the Shroud of Turin features the front and back image of a man who was 5 feet, 9 inches tall. The man was bearded and had shoulder-length hair parted down the middle.

Dark stains on the Shroud are consistent with blood from a crucifixion.

First publicly displayed in 1357, the Shroud of Turin has apparent ties to the Knights of Templar. At the time of its first showing, the Shroud was in the hands of the family of Geoffrey de Charney, a Templar who had been burned at the stake in 1314 along with Jacques de Molay. Some accounts say it was the Knights who removed the cloth from Constantinople, where it was kept safely throughout the 13th century.

Some believe the Shroud of Turin is the cloth that Jesus was wrapped in after his death. All four gospels mention that the body of Jesus was covered in a linen cloth prior to the resurrection. Others assert that the cloth shrouded Jacques de Molay after he was tortured by being nailed to a door.

Still others contend that the Shroud was the early photographic experiments of Leonardo da Vinci. He mentioned working with "optics" in some of his diaries and wrote his notes in a sort of mirrored handwriting style, some say, to keep his experiments secret from the church.

Is the Shroud of Turin authentic? In 1988, scientists using carbon-dating concluded that the material in the Shroud was from around AD 1260 to 1390, which excludes the possibility that the Shroud bears the image of Jesus.

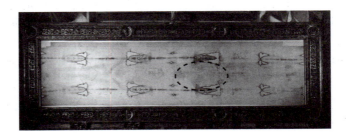

AN UNDERGROUND MYSTERY: THE HOLLOW EARTH THEORY

For centuries, people have believed that Earth is hollow. They claim that civilizations may live inside Earth's core or that it might be a landing base for alien spaceships. This sounds like fantasy, but believers point to startling evidence, including explorers' reports and modern photos taken from space.

A PRIZE INSIDE?

Hollow Earth believers agree that our planet is a shell between 500 and 800 miles thick, and inside that shell is another world. It may be a gaseous realm, an alien outpost, or home to a utopian society.

Some believers add a spiritual spin. Calling the interior world Agartha or Shambhala, they use concepts from Eastern religions and point to ancient legends supporting these ideas.

Many Hollow Earth enthusiasts are certain that people from the outer and inner worlds can visit each other by traveling through openings in the outer shell. One such entrance is a hole in the ocean near the North Pole. A November 1968 photo by the ESSA-7 satellite showed a dark, circular area at the North Pole that was surrounded by ice fields.

Another hole supposedly exists in Antarctica. Some Hollow Earth enthusiasts say Hitler believed that Antarctica held the true opening to Earth's core. Leading Hollow Earth researchers such as Dennis Crenshaw suggest that President Roosevelt ordered the 1939 South Pole expedition to find the entrance before the Germans did.

The poles may not hold the only entrances to a world hidden deep beneath our feet. Jules Verne's famous novel *Journey to the Center of the Earth* supported yet another theory about passage between the worlds. In his story, there were many access points, including waterfalls and inactive volcanoes. Edgar Allan Poe and Edgar Rice Burroughs also wrote about worlds inside Earth. Their ideas were based on science as well as fantasy.

SCIENTISTS TAKE NOTE

Many scientists have taken the Hollow Earth theory seriously. One of the most noted was English astronomer Edmund Halley, of Halley's Comet fame. In 1692, he declared that our planet is hollow, and as evidence, he pointed to global shifts in Earth's magnetic fields, which frequently cause compass anomalies. According to Halley, those shifts could be explained by the movement of rotating worlds inside Earth. In addition, he claimed that the source of gravity—still debated in the 21st century—could be an interior world.

In Halley's opinion, Earth is made of three separate layers or shells, each rotating independently around a solid core. We live on the outer shell, but the inner worlds might be inhabited, too.

Halley also suggested that Earth's interior atmospheres are luminous. We supposedly see them as gas leaking out of Earth's fissures. At the poles, that gas creates the aurora borealis.

SCIENTISTS LOOK DEEPER

Hollow Earth researchers claim that the groundwork for their theories was laid by some of the most notable scientific minds of the 17th and 18th centuries. Although their beliefs remain controversial and largely unsubstantiated, they are still widely discussed and have a network of enthusiasts.

Some researchers claim that Leonhard Euler (1707–1783), one of the greatest mathematicians of all time, believed that Earth's interior includes a glowing core that illuminates life for a well-developed civilization, much like the sun lights our world. Another mathematician, Sir John Leslie (1766–1832), suggested that Earth has a thin crust and also believed the interior cavity was filled with light.

In 1818, a popular lecturer named John Cleves Symmes, Jr., proposed an expedition to prove the Hollow Earth theory. He believed that he could sail to the North Pole, and upon reaching the opening to Earth's core, he could steer his ship over the lip of the entrance, which he believed resembled a waterfall. Then he would continue sailing on waters inside the planet. In 1822 and 1823, Symmes petitioned Congress to fund the expedition, but he was turned down. He died in 1829, and his gravestone in Hamilton, Ohio, is decorated with his model of the Hollow Earth.

PROOF GETS WOOLLY AND WEIRD

In 1846, a remarkably well-preserved—and long extinct—woolly mammoth was found frozen in Siberia. Most woolly mammoths died out about 12,000 years ago, so researchers were baffled by its pristine condition.

Hollow Earth enthusiasts say there is only one explanation: The mammoth lived inside Earth, where those beasts are not extinct. The beast had probably become lost, emerged into our world, and froze to death shortly before the 1846 discovery.

EYEWITNESSES AT THE NORTH POLE

Several respected scientists and explorers have visited the poles and returned with stories that suggest a hollow Earth.

At the start of the 20th century, Arctic explorers Dr. Frederick A. Cook and Rear Admiral Robert E. Peary sighted land—not just an icy wasteland—at the North Pole. Peary first described it as "the white summits of a distant land." A 1913 Arctic expedition also reported seeing "hills, valleys, and snow-capped peaks." All of these claims were dismissed as mirages but would later be echoed by the research of Admiral Richard E.Byrd, the first man to fly over the North Pole. Hollow Earth believers suggest that Byrd actually flew into the interior world and then out again, without realizing it. They cite Byrd's notes as evidence, as he describes his navigational instruments and compasses spinning out of control.

UNIDENTIFIED SUBMERGED OBJECTS

Support for the Hollow Earth theory has also come from UFO enthusiasts. People who study UFOs have also been documenting USOs, or unidentified submerged objects. These mysterious vehicles have been spotted—mostly at sea—since the 19th century.

USOs look like "flying saucers," but instead of vanishing into the skies, they plunge beneath the surface of the ocean. Some are luminous and fly upward from the sea at a fantastic speed...and without making a sound.

UFO enthusiasts believe that these spaceships are visiting worlds beneath the sea. Some are certain that these are actually underwater alien bases. Other UFO researchers think that the ocean conceals entries to a hollow Earth, where the aliens maintain outposts.

THE SEARCH CONTINUES

Scientists have determined that the most likely location for a northern opening to Earth's interior is at 84.4 N Latitude, 141 E Longitude. It's a spot near Siberia, about

600 miles from the North Pole. Photos taken by Apollo 8 in 1968 and Apollo 16 in 1972 show dark, circular areas confirming the location.

Some scientists are studying seismic tomography, which uses natural and human-made explosions as well as earthquakes and other seismic waves to chart Earth's interior masses. So far, scientists confirm that Earth is comprised of three separate layers. And late 20th-century images may suggest a magnificent mountain range at Earth's core.

What may seem like fantasy from a Jules Verne novel could turn out to be an astonishing reality. Hollow Earth societies around the world continue to look for proof of this centuries-old legend…and who knows how it might end.

HEAD LIKE A HOLE: THE WEIRD HISTORY OF TREPANATION

There aren't many medical procedures more than 7,000 years old that are still practiced today. Trepanation, or the practice of drilling a hole in the skull, is one of the few.

AN ANCIENT PRACTICE

Has anyone ever angrily accused you of having a hole in your head? Well, it's not necessarily an exaggeration. Trepanation (also known as trephination) is the practice of boring into the skull and removing a piece of bone, thereby leaving a hole. It is derived from the Greek word *trypanon*, meaning "to bore." This practice was performed by the ancient Greeks, Romans, and Egyptians, among others.

Hippocrates, considered the father of medicine, indicated that the Greeks might have used trepanation to treat head injuries. However, evidence of trepanning without accompanying head trauma has been found in less advanced civilizations; speculation abounds as to its exact purpose and origin. Since the head was considered a barometer for a person's behavior, one theory is that trepanation was used as a way to treat headaches, depression, and other conditions that had no outward trauma signs. Think of it like a pressure release valve: The hole gave evil spirits inside the skull a way out of the body. When the spirits were gone, it was hoped, the symptoms would disappear.

HOW TO TREPAN

In trepanning, the Greeks used an instrument called a terebra, an extremely sharp piece of wood with another piece of wood mounted crossways on it as a handle and attached by a thong. The handle was twisted until the thong was extremely tight. When released, the thong unwound, which spun the sharp piece of wood around and drove it into the skull like a drill. Although it's possible that the terebra was used for a single hole, it is more likely that it was used to make a circular pattern of multiple small holes, thereby making it easier to remove a large piece of bone. Since formal anesthesia had not yet been invented, it is unknown whether any kind of numbing agent was used before trepanation was performed.

The Incas were also adept at trepanation. The procedure was performed using a ceremonial tumi knife made of flint or copper. The surgeon held the patient's head between his knees and rubbed the tumi blade back and forth along the surface of the skull to create four incisions in a crisscross pattern. When the incisions were sufficiently deep, the square-shaped piece of bone in the center was pulled out. Come to think of it, perhaps the procedure hurt more than the symptom.

TREPANATION TODAY

Just when you thought it was safe to assume that the medical field has come so far, hold on—doctors still use this procedure, only now it's called a craniotomy. The underlying methodology is similar: It still involves removing a piece of skull to get to the underlying tissue. The bone is replaced when the procedure is done. If it is not replaced, the operation is called a craniectomy. That procedure is used in many different circumstances, such as for treating a tumor or infection.

However, good ol'-fashion trepanation still has its supporters. One in particular is Bart Hughes, who believes that trepanning can elevate one to a higher state of consciousness. According to Hughes, once man started to walk upright, the brain lost blood because the heart had to frantically pump it throughout the body in a struggle against gravity. Thus, the brain had to shut down certain areas that were not critically needed to assure proper blood flow to vital regions.

Increased blood flow to the brain can elevate a person's consciousness, Hughes reasoned, and he advocated ventilating the skull as a means of making it easier for the heart to send blood to the brain. (Standing on one's head also accomplishes this, but that's just a temporary measure.) Some of his followers have actually performed trepanation on themselves. For better or gross, a few have even filmed the process. In 2001, two men from Utah pled guilty to practicing medicine without a license after they had bored holes into a woman's skull to treat her chronic fatigue and depression. There's no word as to whether the procedure actually worked, or if she's just wearing a lot of hats nowadays.

THE VANISHING TREASURE ROOM

In the Age of Enlightenment, kings and emperors built immense palaces to outdo one another—each one bigger and more gilded and bejeweled than the last. But one of Russia's greatest 18th-century treasures became one of the 20th century's greatest unsolved mysteries.

The storied history of the Amber Room begins in 1701, when it was commissioned by Frederick I of Prussia. Cosidered by admirers and artists alike to be the "Eighth Wonder of the World," the sparkling, honey-gold room consisted of wall panels inlaid with prehistoric amber, finely carved and illuminated by candles and mirrors. In 1716, Prussian King Freidrich Wilhelm I gifted the panels to then-ally Russian Tsar Peter the Great to ornament the imperial palace at his new capital, St. Petersburg.

After sitting at the Winter Palace for four decades, the Amber Room was moved to Tsarskoye Selo, the Romanov palace just south of St. Petersburg. During the mid-18th century, Prussia's King Frederick the Great sent Russia's Empress Elizabeth more of the amber matrial from his Baltic holdings, and Elizabeth ordered her court's great Italian architect, Bartolomeo Rastrelli, to expand the Amber Room into an 11-foot- square masterpiece.

The golden room was not finished until 1770, under the reign of Catherine the Great. Incorporating more than six tons of amber and accented with semiprecious stones, the fabled room became not only a prized jewel of the Russian empire, but a symbol of the long-standing alliance between Prussia and Russia.

FROM PEACE TO WAR

Two centuries after the Amber Room was removed to the Catherine Palace, the world was a much darker place.

Prussia and Russia, formerly faithful allies, were locked in a deadly struggle that would bring down both imperial houses. By 1941, the former dominions of Frederick and Peter were ruled by Adolf Hitler and Joseph Stalin.

In a surprise attack, Hitler's armies drove across the Soviet border in June 1941 to launch the most destructive war in history. German panzers drove from the Polish frontier to the gates of Moscow in an epic six-month campaign, devouring some of the most fertile, productive territory in Eastern Europe.

One of the unfortunate cities in the path of the Nazi onslaught was St. Petersburg, renamed Leningrad by its communist masters. Frantic palace curators desperately tried to remove the Amber Room's antique panels, but the brittle prehistoric resin began to crumble as the panels were detached. Faced with probable destruction of one of Russia's greatest treasures or its abandonment to the Nazis, the curators attempted to hide the room's precious panels by covering them with gauze and wallpaper.

Although Leningrad withstood a long, bloody siege, German troops swept through the city's suburbs, capturing Tsarskoye Selo intact in October 1941. Soldiers discovered the treasure hidden behind the wallpaper, and German troops disassembled the room's panels over a 36-hour period, packed them in 27 crates, and shipped them back to Königsberg, in East Prussia.

The fabled Amber Room panels were put on display in Königsberg's castle museum.They remained there for two years—until the Third Reich began to crumble before the weight of Soviet and Anglo-American military forces. Sometime in 1944, the room's valuable panels were allegedly dismantled and packed into crates, to prevent damage by British and Soviet bombers. In January 1945,

Hitler permitted the westward movement of cultural treasures, including the Italo-Russo-German masterpiece.

And from there, the Amber Room was lost to history.

THE GREAT TREASURE HUNT

The world was left to speculate about the fate of the famous imperial room, and dozens of theories have been spawned about the room's whereabouts. Some claim the Amber Room was lost—sunk aboard a submarine, bombed to pieces, or perhaps burned in Königsberg. This last conclusion was accepted by Alexander Brusov, a Soviet investigator sent to find the Amber Room shortly after the war's end. Referring to the destruction of Königsberg Castle by Red Army forces on April 9, 1945, he concluded: "Summarizing all the facts, we can say that the Amber Room was destroyed between 9 and 11 April 1945." An in-depth hunt by two British investigative journalists pieced together the last days of the Amber Room and concluded that its fate was sealed when Soviet troops accidentally set fire to the castle compound during the last month of combat, destroying the brittle jewels and obscuring their location.

Other treasure hunters, however, claim the room still sits in an abandoned mine shaft or some long-forgotten Nazi bunker beneath the outskirts of Königsberg. One German investigator claimed former SS officers told him the room's panels were packed up and hidden in an abandoned silver mine near Berlin; a Lithuanian official claimed witnesses saw SS troops hiding the panels in a local swamp. Neither has been able to prove his claims.

THE TRAIL GOES COLD

The hunt for the Amber Room has been made more difficult because its last witnesses are gone—several under mysterious circumstances. The Nazi curator in charge of the room died of typhus the day before he was scheduled to be interviewed by the KGB, and a Soviet intelligence officer who spoke to a journalist about the room's whereabouts died the following day in a car crash. In 1987, Georg Stein, a former German soldier who had devoted his life to searching for the Amber Room, was found murdered in a forest, his stomach slit open by a scalpel.

In 1997, the world got a tantalizing glimpse of the long-lost treasure when German police raided the office of a Bremen lawyer who was attempting to sell an amber mosaic worth $2.5 million on behalf of one of his clients, the son of a former German lieutenant. The small mosaic—inlaid with jade and onyx as well as amber—had been stolen from the Amber Room by a German officer and was separated from the main panels. After its seizure, this last true remnant of the legendary tsarist treasure made its way back to Russia in April 2000.

Decades of searches by German and Soviet investigators have come up empty. The fate of the fabled room—worth an estimated $142 million to $250 million in today's currency—has remained an elusive ghost for treasure seekers, mystery writers, and investigators looking for the Holy Grail of Russian baroque artwork.

PICKING UP THE PIECES

In 1979, the Soviet government, with help from a donation made by a German gas firm in 1999, began amassing old photographs of the Amber Room and pieces of the rare amber to create a reconstructed room worthy of its predecessor. Carefully rebuilt at a cost exceeding $7 million, the reconstructed room was dedicated by the Russian president and German chancellor at a ceremony in

2003, marking the tri-centennial of St. Petersburg's founding. The dazzling Amber Room is now on display for the thousands of tourists who come to Tsarskoye Selo to view the playground of one of Europe's great dynasties.

THE BARD VS. BACON: WHO WROTE SHAKESPEARE?

"What's in a name? That which we call a rose, by any other name, would smell as sweet." But would that which we call prose, by any other name, read as neat?

The quote above was penned by William Shakespeare—or was it? Many scholars have raised doubts as to whether he really wrote some of the finest words in Western literature. Did other writers actually do the deed? Both sides believe they have the evidence to prove their point.

MEET BILL

William Shakespeare was born in Stratford-upon-Avon, England, in April 1564—the exact date is unknown. Many details of his life are vague, which has fueled the rampant speculation about authorship. It is generally accepted that he was the first in his family to read and write, although the extent of his education is unknown. His father was involved in local politics, so it  is likely that Shakespeare attended school to study Latin and literature. At age 18, Shakespeare married Anne Hathaway, who was eight years older than he was and three months pregnant with their first child, Susanna. Twins Hamnet and Judith were born two years later.

The Bard's life story seems to disappear into the mist for more than seven years at this point, resurfacing in 1592, when he became involved in London theater. As a playwright and actor, he founded a performing troupe that was soon part of the court of King James I. Shakespeare retired in 1613, returning to his hometown with some wealth. He died in 1616 and was laid to rest in the Holy Trinity Church of Stratford-upon-Avon.

THE PLAY'S THE THING

While Shakespeare's plays were performed during his lifetime, they were not collected and published in book form until seven years after his death; The First Folio contained 36 of his theatrical works. Editors John Heminge and Henry Condell categorized the plays as tragedies, comedies, and histories. Many of Shakespeare's works, such as *Hamlet* and *King Lear*, were based on writings of former playwrights or even of Shakespeare's contemporaries—a common practice of the time. He also penned more than 150 sonnets, which often focused on love or beauty.

The diversity of this amazing body of work is what leads many to wonder whether Shakespeare had the education or ability to write it all. Certainly, they insist, others with better backgrounds and academic credentials were more likely to have actually written such great and timeless works of literature. Furthermore, they say, many of the plays displayed the acumen of a well-traveled writer—something Shakespeare was most likely not—someone who had a great knowledge of foreign languages, geography, and local customs. Who could have written such worldly plays?

BRINGING HOME THE BACON

Francis Bacon was born into a royal London family in 1561. Fragile as a young child, Bacon was schooled at home. He spent three years at Trinity College at Cambridge and traveled to Paris at age 15. Bacon became a lawyer and a member of the British Parliament in 1584. He soon joined the court of Queen Elizabeth and was knighted by King James I in 1603. Bacon eventually ascended to the positions of solicitor general and attorney general of the British government. He died of bronchitis in 1626.

Bacon is best remembered for his part in developing the scientific method, a process of systematic investigation. This standard prescribes defining a question, performing diligent research about the subject, forming a hypothesis, experimenting and collecting data, analyzing the results, and developing a conclusion. The progression has become commonplace in all types of scientific work, from grade school projects to research labs, and is still used today. But the multitalented Bacon was also a writer and essayist who once observed that "knowledge is power." His works include *Novum Organum*, *Astrologia Sana*, and *Meditationes Sacrae*. But could the man who penned these works be diverse and capable enough to also write *Much Ado About Nothing*, *Romeo and Juliet*, and words such as "If music be the food of love, play on"?

SOMETHING IS ROTTEN IN THE STATE OF... AUTHORSHIP

Speculation about the origin of Shakespeare's work began in the mid-1800s, as writers and scholars sought to demystify the works of the Bard. By the early 1900s, even the great American humorist Mark Twain had weighed in and questioned the authenticity of Shakespeare's plays and sonnets, albeit in his own way.

In *Is Shakespeare Dead?*, Twain parodied those intellectuals who tried to discredit the man from Stratford-upon-Avon. The satiric piece questioned how biographers could write such detailed stories about their subject when so little solid information existed in the first place. But Twain also raised the question of whether Shakespeare could even write.

Similarities between the writings of Shakespeare and Bacon are abundant, and perhaps a bit too coincidental. For example, Shakespeare's Hamlet offers, "To thine own self be true,...Thou canst not then be false to any man." In "Essay of Wisdom," Bacon wrote, "Be so true to thyself as thou be not false to others." Plagiarism? Who can really say? In *Julius Caesar*, Shakespeare wrote, "Cowards die many times before their deaths." In Bacon's "Essay of Friendship," he offered, "Men have their time, and die many times." Coincidence? Sure, maybe. The Bard wrote, "Tomorrow, and tomorrow, and tomorrow/Creeps in this petty pace from day to day" in *Macbeth*. Bacon observed in *Religious Meditations*, "The Spanish have a proverb, 'To-morrow, to-morrow; and when to-morrow comes, tomorrow.'" Is it possible that Shakespeare knew of the same Spanish proverb? Certainly. While other similarities and questions proliferate, enough disbelief and lack of concrete evidence remain to thrill the world's doubting Thomases.

PARTING IS SUCH SWEET SORROW

Amid the swirl of controversy, most academics are convinced that Shakespeare himself wrote the plays and sonnets that made him famous. Of course, that conviction has done little to discourage those who have their doubts.

CIRCLE MARKS THE SPOT: THE MYSTERY OF CROP CIRCLES

The result of cyclonic winds? Attempted alien communication? Evidence of hungry cows with serious OCD? There are many theories as to how crop circles, or grain stalks flattened in recognizable patterns, have come to exist. Most people dismiss them as pranks, but there are more than a few who believe there's something otherworldly going on.

YE OLE CROP CIRCLE

Some experts believe the first crop circles date back to the late 1600s, but there isn't much evidence to support them. Other experts cite evidence of more than 400 simple circles 6 to 20 feet in diameter that appeared worldwide hundreds of years ago. The kinds of circles they refer to are still being found today, usually after huge, cyclonic thunderstorms pass over a large expanse of agricultural land. These circles are much smaller and not nearly as precise as the geometric, mathematically complex circles that started cropping up in the second half of the 20th century. Still, drawings and writings about these smaller circles lend weight to the claims of believers that the crop circle phenomenon isn't a new thing. The International Crop Circle Database reports stories of "UFO nests" in British papers during the 1960s. About a decade or so later, crop circles fully captured the attention (and the imagination) of the masses.

NO, VIRGINIA, THERE AREN'T ANY ALIENS

In 1991, two men from Southampton, England, came forward with a confession. Doug Bower and Dave Chorley admitted that they were responsible for the majority of the crop circles found in England during the preceding two decades.

Inspired by stories of "UFO nests" in the 1960s, the two decided to add a little excitement to their sleepy town. With boards, string, and a few simple navigational tools, the men worked through the night to create complex patterns in fields that could be seen from the road. It worked, and before long, much of the Western world was caught up in crop circle fever. Some claimed it was irrefutable proof that UFOs were landing on Earth. Others said God was trying to communicate with humans "through the language of mathematics." For believers, there was no doubt that supernatural or extraterrestrial forces were at work. But skeptics were thrilled to hear the confession from Bower and Chorley, since they never believed the circles to be anything but a prank in the first place.

Before the men came forward, more crop circles appeared throughout the 1980s and '90s, many of them not made by Bower and Chorley. Circles "mysteriously" occurred in Australia, Canada, the United States, Argentina, India, and even Afghanistan. In 1995, more than 200 cases of crop circles were reported worldwide. In 2001, a formation that appeared in Wiltshire, England, contained 409 circles and covered more than 12 acres.

Many were baffled that anyone could believe these large and admittedly rather intricate motifs were anything but human-made. Plus, the more media coverage crop circles garnered, then more new crop circles appeared. Other people came forward, admitting that they were the "strange and unexplained power" behind the circles. Even then, die-hard believers dismissed the hoaxers, vehemently suggesting that they were either players in a government cover-up, captives of aliens forced to throw everyone off track, or just average Joes looking for 15 minutes of fame by claiming to have made something that was clearly the work of nonhumans.

Scientists were deployed to ascertain the facts. In 1999, a well-funded team of experts was assembled to examine numerous crop circles in the UK. The verdict? At least 80 percent of the circles were, beyond a shadow of a doubt, created by humans. Footprints, abandoned tools, and video of a group of hoaxers caught in the act all debunked the theory that crop circles were created by aliens.

BUT STILL...

So if crop circles are nothing more than hoaxers having fun or artists playing with aunique medium, why are we still so interested? Movies such as *Signs* in 2002 capitalized on the public's fascination with the phenomenon, and crop circles still capture headlines. Skeptics will scoff, but from time to time, there is a circle that doesn't quite fit the profile of a human-made prank.

There have been claims that fully functional cell phones cease to work once the caller steps inside certain crop circles. Could it be caused by some funky ion-scramble emitted by an extraterrestrial force? Some researchers have tried to re-create the circles and succeeded, but only with the use of high-tech tools and equipment that wouldn't be available to the average prankster. If all of these circles were made by humans, why are so few people busted for trespassing in the middle of the night? And where are all the footprints?

Eyewitness accounts of UFOs rising from fields can hardly be considered irrefutable evidence, but there are several reports from folks who swear they saw ships, lights, and movement in the sky just before crop circles were discovered.

MYSTERIOUS DISAPPEARANCES IN THE BERMUDA TRIANGLE

The Bermuda Triangle is an infamous stretch of the Atlantic Ocean bordered by Florida, Bermuda, and Puerto Rico where strange disappearances have occurred throughout history. The Coast Guard doesn't recognize the Triangle or the supernatural explanations for the mysterious disappearances. There are some probable causes for the missing vessels—hurricanes, undersea earthquakes, and magnetic fields that interfere with compasses and other positioning devices. But it's much more interesting to think they were sucked into another dimension, abducted by aliens, or simply vanished into thin air.

FLIGHT 19

On the afternoon of December 5, 1945, five Avenger torpedo bombers left the Naval Air Station at Fort Lauderdale, Florida, with Lt. Charles Taylor in command of a crew of 13 student pilots. About 90 minutes into the flight, Taylor radioed the base to say that his compasses weren't working, but he figured he was somewhere over the Florida Keys. The lieutenant who received the signal told Taylor to fly north toward Miami, as long as he was sure he was actually over the Keys. Although he was an experienced pilot, Taylor got horribly turned around, and the more he tried to get out of the Keys, the further out to sea he and his crew traveled. As night fell, radio signals worsened, until, finally, there was nothing at all from Flight 19. A U.S. Navy investigation reported that Taylor's confusion caused the disaster, but his mother convinced them to change the official report to read that the planes went down for "causes unknown." The planes have never been recovered.

THE *SPRAY*

Joshua Slocum, the first man to sail solo around the world, never should have been lost at sea, but it appears that's exactly what happened. In 1909, the *Spray* left the East Coast of the United States for Venezuela via the Caribbean Sea. Slocum was never heard from or seen again and was declared dead in 1924. The ship was solid, and Slocum was a pro, so nobody knows what happened. Perhaps he was felled by a larger ship or maybe he was taken down by pirates. No one knows for sure that Slocum disappeared within the Triangle's waters, but Bermuda buffs claim Slocum's story as part of the area's mysterious and supernatural legacy.

STAR TIGER

The *Star Tiger*, commanded by Capt. B. W. McMillan, was flying from England to Bermuda in early 1948. On January 30, McMillan said he expected to arrive in Bermuda at 5:00 a.m., but neither he nor any of the 31 people onboard the *Star Tiger* were ever heard from again. When the Civil Air Ministry launched an investigation, they learned that the S.S. *Troubadour* had reported seeing a low-flying aircraft halfway between Bermuda and the entrance to Delaware Bay. If that aircraft was the *Star Tiger*, it was drastically off course. According to the Civil Air Ministry, the fate of the *Star Tiger* remains unknown.

STAR ARIEL

On January 17, 1949, a Tudor IV aircraft like the *Star Tiger* left Bermuda with seven crew members and 13 passengers en route to Jamaica. That morning, Capt. J.

C. McPhee reported that the flight was going smoothly. Shortly afterward, another more cryptic message came from the captain, when he reported that he was changing his frequency, and then nothing more was heard— ever. More than 60 aircraft and 13,000 people were deployed to look for the *Star Ariel*, but no hint of debris or wreckage was ever found. After the *Star Ariel* disappeared, production of Tudor IVs ceased.

FLIGHT 201

This Cessna left for Fort Lauderdale on March 31, 1984, en route for Bimini Island in the Bahamas, but it never made it. Not quite midway to its destination, the plane slowed its airspeed significantly, but no distress signals came from the plane. Suddenly, the plane dropped from the air into the water, completely vanishing from the radar. A woman on Bimini Island swore she saw a plane plunge into the sea about a mile offshore, but no wreckage has ever been found.

TEIGNMOUTH ELECTRON

Who said that the Bermuda Triangle only swallows up ships and planes? Who's to say it can't also make a man go mad? Perhaps that's what happened on the *Teignmouth Electron* in 1969. The *Sunday Times* Golden Globe race of 1968 left England on October 31 and required each contestant to sail his ship solo. Donald Crowhurst was one of the entrants, but he never made it to the finish line. The *Teignmouth Electron* was found abandoned in the middle of the Bermuda Triangle in July 1969. Logbooks recovered from the ship reveal that Crowhurst was deceiving organizers about his position in the race and going a little bit nutty out there in the big blue ocean. The last entry of his log was dated June 29—it is believed that Crowhurst jumped overboard and drowned himself in the Triangle.

GONE WITHOUT A TRACE

While we all watch in amazement as magicians make everything from small coins to giant buildings disappear, in our hearts, we all know it's a trick. Things don't just disappear, especially not people. Or do they?

LOUIS LE PRINCE

The name Louis Aimé Augustin Le Prince doesn't mean much to most people, but some believe he was the first person to record moving images on film, a good seven years before Thomas Edison. Whether or not he did so is open to debate, as is what happened to him on September 16, 1890. On that day, Le Prince's brother accompanied him to the train station in Dijon, France, where he was scheduled to take the express train to Paris. When the train reached Paris, however, Le Prince and his luggage were nowhere to be found. The train was searched, as were the tracks between Dijon and Paris, but no sign of Le Prince or his luggage was ever found. Theories about his disappearance range from his being murdered for trying to fight Edison over the patent of the first motion picture to his family forcing him to go into hiding to keep him safe from people who wanted his patents for themselves. Others believe that Le Prince took his own life because he was nearly bankrupt.

DOROTHY ARNOLD

After spending most of December 12, 1910, shopping in Manhattan, American socialite Dorothy Arnold told a friend she was planning to walk home through Central Park. She never made it. Fearing their daughter had eloped with her one-time boyfriend George Griscom, Jr., the Arnolds immediately hired the Pinkerton Detective Agency, although they did not report her missing to police until almost a month later. Once the press heard the news, theories spread like wildfire, most of them pointing the finger at Griscom. Some believed he had murdered Arnold, but others thought she had died as the result of a botched abortion. Still others felt her family had banished her to Switzerland and then used her disappearance as a cover-up. No evidence was ever found to formally charge Griscom, and Arnold's disappearance remains unsolved.

D. B. COOPER

On the evening of November 24, 1971, a man calling himself Dan Cooper (later known as D. B. Cooper) hijacked an airplane, and demanded $200,000 and four parachutes, which he received when the plane landed in Seattle. Cooper allowed the plane's passengers to disembark but then ordered the pilot to fly to Mexico. Once the plane had gained enough altitude, somewhere over the Cascade Mountains near Woodland, Washington, Cooper jumped from the plane and fell into history. Despite a massive manhunt, no trace of him has ever been found. In 1980, an eight-year-old boy found nearly $6,000 in rotting $20 bills lying along the banks of the Columbia River. A check of their serial numbers found that they were part of the ransom money given to Cooper, but what became Cooper, is a mystery.

FREDERICK VALENTICH

To vanish without a trace is rather unusual. But to vanish in an airplane while chasing a UFO—now that's unique. Yet that's exactly what happened to 20-year-old pilot Frederick Valentich on the night of October 21, 1978. Shortly after 7:00 p.m., while flying a Cessna 182L to King Island, Australia, Valentich radioed that an "unidentified craft" was hovering over his plane. For the next several minutes, he attempted to describe the object, which had blinking lights and was "not an aircraft."

At approximately 7:12 a.m., Valentich stated that he was having engine trouble. Immediately after that, the flight tower picked up 17 seconds of "metallic, scraping sounds." Then all was silent. A search began immediately, but no trace of Valentich or his plane was ever found. Strangely enough, the evening Valentich disappeared, there were numerous reports of UFOs seen all over the skies of Australia.

FRANK MORRIS, JOHN ANGLIN, AND CLARENCE ANGLIN

Officially, records show that there was never a successful escape from Alcatraz Prison while it was in operation. Of course, those records leave out the part that three men might have made it, but they disappeared in the process.

After spending two years planning their escape, inmates Frank Morris and brothers Clarence and John Anglin placed homemade dummies in their bunks, crawled through hand-dug tunnels, and made their way to the prison roof. Then they apparently climbed down, hopped aboard homemade rafts, and made their way out into San Francisco Bay.

The next day, one of the largest manhunts in history began. Pieces of a raft and a life preserver were found floating in the bay, as well as a bag containing personal items from the escapees, but that was all. The official report stated that in all likelihood, the men drowned. However, a 2003 episode of *Mythbusters* determined that the men may have survived.

SPACE GHOSTS

Shortly after the Soviet Union successfully launched Sputnik 1 on October 4, 1957, rumors swirled that several cosmonauts had died during missions gone horribly wrong, and their spacecraft had drifted out of Earth's orbit and into the vast reaches of the universe.

MOSCOW, DO YOU COPY?

It was easy to believe such stories at the time. After all, the United States was facing off against the Soviet Union in the Cold War, and the thought that the ruthless

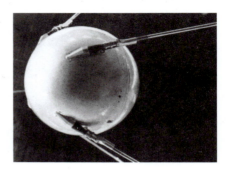

Russians would do anything to win the space race—including sending cosmonauts to their doom—seemed plausible.

However, numerous researchers have investigated the stories and concluded that, though the Soviet space program was far from perfect and some cosmonauts had in fact died, there are no dead cosmonauts floating in space.

According to authors Hal Morgan and Kerry Tucker, the earliest rumors of deceased cosmonauts even mentioned their names and the dates of their doomed missions: Aleksei Ledovsky in 1957, Serenti Shiborin in 1958, and Mirya Gromova in 1959. In fact, by the time Yuri Gagarin became the first human in space in April 1961, the alleged body count exceeded a dozen.

SPACE SPIES

So prevalent were these stories that no less an "authority" than *Reader's Digest* reported on them in its April 1965 issue. Key to the mystery were two brothers in Italy, Achille and Giovanni Battista Judica-Cordiglia, who operated a homemade listening post with a huge dish antenna. Over a seven-month period, the brothers claimed to have overheard radio signals from three troubled Soviet spacecraft:

❖ On November 28, 1960, a Soviet spacecraft supposedly radioed three times, in Morse code and in English, "SOS to the entire world."

❖ In early February 1961, the brothers are alleged to have picked up the sound of a rapidly beating heart and labored breathing, which they interpreted to be the final throes of a dying cosmonaut.

❖ On May 17, 1961, two men and a woman were allegedly overheard saying, in Russian, "Conditions growing worse. Why don't you answer? We are going slower...the world will never know about us."

THE BLACK HOLE OF SOVIET PR

One reason rumors of dead cosmonauts were so believable was the extremely secretive nature of the early Soviet space program. Whereas the United States touted its program as a major advance in science and its astronauts as public heroes, the Soviet Union revealed little about its program or the people involved.

It's not surprising, then, that the Soviet Union did not report to the world the death of Valentin Bondarenko, a cosmonaut who died tragically in a fire after he tossed an alcohol-soaked cotton ball on a hot plate and ignited the oxygen-rich chamber in which he was training. He died in 1961, but it wasn't revealed publicly until 1986.

Adding to the rumors was the fact that other cosmonauts had been mysteriously airbrushed out of official government photographs. However, most had been removed because they had been dropped from the space program for academic, disciplinary, or medical reasons—not because they had died during a mission. One cosmonaut, Grigoriy Nelyubov, was booted from the program in 1961 for engaging in a drunken brawl at a rail station (he died five years later when he stepped in front of a train). Nelyubov's story, like so many others, was not made public until the mid-1980s.

Only one Soviet cosmonaut is known to have died during an actual space mission. In 1967, Vladimir Komarov was killed when the parachute on his Soyuz 1 spacecraft failed to open properly during reentry. A Russian engineer later acknowledged that Komarov's mission had been ordered before the spacecraft had been fully debugged, likely for political reasons.

ONE HECK OF A HOAX? THE MYSTERIOUS VOYNICH MANUSCRIPT

Dubbed the World's Most Mysterious Book, the Voynich manuscript contains more than 200 vellum pages of vivid, colorful illustrations and handwritten prose. There's only one small problem: No one knows what any of it means. Or whether it means anything at all.

It was "discovered" in 1912 after being hidden from the world for almost 250 years. An American antique book dealer named Wilfried Voynich came across the medieval manuscript at an Italian Jesuit College. Approximately nine inches by six inches in size, the manuscript bore a soft, light-brown vellum cover, which was unmarked, untitled, and gave no indication as to when it had been written or by whom.

Bound inside were approximately 230 yellow parchment pages, most of which contained richly colored drawings of strange plants, celestial bodies, and other scientific matter. Many of the pages were adorned by naked nymphs bathing in odd-looking plumbing and personal-size washtubs. Handwritten text written in flowing script accompanied the illustrations.

Although Voynich was an expert antiquarian, he was baffled by the book's contents. And today—nearly a century later—the manuscript that came to bear his name remains a mystery.

WEIRD SCIENCE

The mystery surrounding the Voynich manuscript begins with its content, which reads (so to speak) like a work of weird science presented in six identifiable "sections":

❖ A botanical section, containing drawings of plants that no botanist has ever been able to identify.

❖ An astronomical section, with illustrations of the sun, moon, stars, and zodiac symbols surrounded by naked nymphs bathing in individual washtubs.

❖ A "biological" section, showing perplexing anatomical drawings of chambers or organs connected by tubes—and which also features more nymphs swimming in their inner liquids.

❖ A cosmological section, consisting mostly of unexplained circular drawings.

❖ A pharmaceutical section, depicting drawings of plant parts (leaves, roots) placed next to containers.

◆ A recipe section, featuring short paragraphs "bulleted" by stars in the margin.

Weirder still are the ubiquitous nymphs—a nice touch perhaps, but how they relate to the subject matter is anyone's guess.

MANY MYSTERIES, STILL NO ANSWERS

And then there's the manuscript's enigmatic text. The world's greatest cryptologists have failed to unravel its meaning. Even the American and British code breakers who cracked the Japanese and German codes in World War II were stumped. To this day, not a single word of the Voynich manuscript has been deciphered.

This, of course, has led to key unsolved questions, most notably:

◆ Who wrote it? A letter found with the manuscript, dated 1666, credits Roger Bacon, a Franciscan friar who lived from 1214 to 1294. This has since been discredited because the manuscript's date of origin is generally considered to be between 1450 and 1500. There are as many theories about who wrote it as there are nymphs among its pages. In fact, some believe Voynich forged the whole thing.

◆ What is it? It was first thought to be a coded description of Bacon's early scientific discoveries. Since then, other theories ranging from an ancient prayer book written in a pidgin Germanic language to one big, elaborate hoax (aside from that supposedly perpetrated by Voynich) have been posited.

◆ Is it real writing? Is the script composed in a variation of a known language, a lost language, an encrypted language, an artificial language? Or is it just plain gibberish?

WHAT DO WE KNOW?

Despite the aura of mystery surrounding the manuscript, it has been possible to trace its travels over the past 400 years. The earliest known owner was Holy Roman Emperor Rudolph II, who purchased it in 1586. By 1666, the manuscript had passed through a series of owners to Athanasius Kircher, a Jesuit scholar who hid it in the college where Voynich found it 250 years later.

After being passed down to various members of Voynich's estate, the manuscript was sold in 1961 to a rare-book collector who sought to resell it for a fortune. After failing to find a buyer, he donated it to Yale University, where it currently resides—still shrouded in mystery—in the Beinecke Rare Book and Manuscript Library.

THE SEARCH FOR MEANING CONTINUES...

To this day, efforts to translate the Voynich manuscript continue. And still, the manuscript refuses to yield its secrets, leading experts to conclude that it's either an ingenious hoax or the ultimate unbreakable code. The hoax theory gained some ground in 2004 when Dr. Gordon Rugg, a computer-science lecturer at Keele University, announced that he had replicated the Voynich manuscript using a low-tech device called a Cardan grille. According to Rugg, this proved that the manuscript was likely a fraud—a volume of jibberish created, perhaps, in an attempt to con money out of Emperor Rudolph II. Mystery solved? Well, it's not quite as simple as that. Many researchers remain unconvinced. Sure, Rugg may have proven that the manuscript might be a hoax. But the possibility that it is not a hoax remains. And thus, the search for meaning continues...

THE DYATLOV PASS INCIDENT

Nine experienced hikers and skiers trek into the Russian wilderness and promptly disappear. Weeks later, their mangled bodies are found among the ruins of the campsite, with no trace of evidence as to how they died. Read on for a closer look at one of the greatest (and creepiest) unsolved mysteries of modern times.

OFF TO THE OTORTEN MOUNTAIN

In early 1959, a group of outdoor enthusiasts formed a skiing and hiking expedition to Otorten Mountain, which is part of the northern Ural Mountain range in Russia. The group, led by Igor Dyatlov, consisted of seven other men and two women: Yury Doroshenko, Georgy Krivonischenko, Alexander Kolevatov, Rustem Slobodin, Nicolas Thibeaux-Brignolle, Yuri Yudin, Alexander Zolotaryov, Lyudmila Dubinina, and Zinaida Kolmogorova. The group's journey began on January 27. The following day, Yudin became ill and had to return home. It would be the last time he would see his friends alive. Using personal photographs and journals belonging to the members of the ski trip to piece together the chain of events, it appeared as though on February 1, the group got disoriented making their way to Otorten Mountain and ended up heading too far to the west. Once they realized they were heading in the wrong direction, the decision was made to simply set up camp for the night. What happened next is a mystery to this day.

MOUNTAIN OF THE DEAD

When no word had been heard from the group by February 20, eight days after their planned return, a group of volunteers organized a search. On February 26, they found the group's abandoned campsite on the east side of the mountain Kholat Syakhl. (As if the story were written by a horror novelist, Kholat Syakhl happens to mean "Mountain of the Dead" in the Mansi language.) The search team found a badly damaged tent that appeared to have been ripped open from the inside. They also found several sets of footprints. Following the trail of footprints, searchers discovered the bodies of Krivonischenko and Doroshenko, shoeless and dressed only in their underwear. Three more bodies—those belonging to Dyatlov, Kolmogorova and Slobodin—were found nearby. It was later determined that all five had died from hypothermia.

On May 4, the bodies of the four other hikers were recovered in the woods near where the bodies of Krivonischenko and Doroshenko had been found. The discovery of these four raised even more questions. To begin with, Thibeaux-Brignolle's skull had been crushed and both Dubunina and Zolotaryov had major chest fractures. The force needed to cause these wounds was compared to that of a high-speed car crash. Oddly, Dubinina's tongue appeared to have been ripped out. Looking at the evidence, it appeared as though all nine members had bedded down for the night, only to be woken up by something so frightening that they all quickly left the tent and ran into the freezing cold night. One by one, they either froze to death or else succumbed to their injuries, the cause of which was never determined.

REMAINS A MYSTERY

Things got even stranger at the funerals for the nine individuals. Family members would later remark that some
of the deceased's skin had become orange and their
hair had turned grey. Medical tests and a Geiger counter
brought to the site showed some of the bodies had high
levels of radiation.

So what happened to the hikers? Authorities eventually
concluded that "an unknown compelling force" caused
the deaths. The case would be officially closed in the
spring of 1959 due to the "absence of a guilty party."
Stories and theories still abound, pointing to everything
from the Russian government covering up secret military
exercises in the area to violent UFO encounters. Today,
the area where the nine hikers met their untimely demise is known as Dyatlov Pass, after the leader of the
ill-fated group.

CHAPTER 2
UNSOLVED MURDERS

THE BLACK DAHLIA MURDER MYSTERY

One of the most baffling murder mysteries in U.S. history began innocently enough on the morning of January 15, 1947. Betty Bersinger was walking with her young daughter in the Leimert Park area of Los Angeles, when she spotted something lying in a vacant lot that caused her blood to run cold. She ran to a nearby house and called the police. Officers Wayne Fitzgerald and Frank Perkins arrived on the scene shortly after 11:00 a.m.

A GRISLY DISCOVERY

Lying only several feet from the road, in plain sight, was the naked body of a young woman. Her body had numerous cuts and abrasions, including a knife wound from ear to ear that resembled a ghoulish grin. Even more horrific was that her body had been completely severed at the midsection, and the two halves had been placed as if they were part of some morbid display. That's what disturbed officers the most: The killer appeared to have carefully posed the victim close to the street because he wanted people to find his grotesque handiwork.

Something else that troubled the officers was that even though the body had been brutally violated and desecrated, there was very little blood found at the scene. The only blood evidence recovered was a possible bloody footprint and an empty cement package with a spot of blood on it. In fact, the body was so clean that it appeared to have just been washed.

Shortly before removing the body, officers scoured the area for a possible murder weapon, but none was recovered. A coroner later determined that the cause of death was from hemorrhage and shock due to a concussion of the brain and lacerations of the face, probably from a very large knife.

POSITIVE IDENTIFICATION

After a brief investigation, police were able to identify the deceased as Elizabeth Short, who was born in Hyde Park, Massachusetts, on July 29, 1924. At age 19, Short had moved to California to live with her father, but she moved out and spent the next few years moving back and forth between California, Florida, and Massachusetts. In July 1946, Short returned to California to see Lt. Gordon Fickling, a former boyfriend, who was stationed in Long Beach. For the last six months of her life, Short lived in an assortment of hotels, rooming houses, and private homes. She was last seen a week before her body was found, which made police very interested in finding out where and with whom she spent her final days.

THE BLACK DAHLIA IS BORN

As police continued their investigation, reporters jumped all over the story and began referring to the unknown killer by names such as "sex-crazed maniac" and even "werewolf." Short herself was also given a nickname: the Black Dahlia. Reporters said it was a name friends had called her as a play on the movie *The Blue Dahlia*, which had recently been released. However, others contend Short was never called the Black Dahlia while she was alive; it was just something reporters made up for a better story. Either way, it wasn't long before newspapers around the globe were splashing front-page headlines about the horrific murder of the Black Dahlia.

THE KILLER IS STILL OUT THERE

As time wore on, hundreds of police officers were assigned to the Black Dahlia investigation. They combed the streets, interviewing people and following leads. Although police interviewed thousands of potential suspects—and dozens even confessed to the murder—to this day, no one has ever officially been charged with the crime. After 70 years and several books and movies after the crime, the Elizabeth Short murder case is still listed as "open." We are no closer to knowing who killed Short or why than when her body was first discovered.

There is one bright note to this story. In February 1947, perhaps as a result of the Black Dahlia case, the state of California became the first state to pass a law requiring all convicted sex offenders to register themselves.

THE LIZZIE BORDEN MURDER MYSTERY

Most people know the rhyme that begins, "Lizzie Borden took an axe and gave her mother 40 whacks…" In reality, approximately 20 hatchet chops cut down Abby Borden, but no matter the number, Lizzie's stepmother was very much dead on that sultry August morning in 1892. Lizzie's father, Andrew, was killed about an hour later. His life was cut short by about a dozen hatchet chops to the head. No one knows who was guilty of these murders, but Lizzie has always carried the burden of suspicion.

ANDREW BORDEN, AN AMERICAN "SCROOGE"

Andrew Jackson Borden had been one of the richest men in Fall River, Massachusetts, with a net worth of nearly half a million dollars. In 1892, that was enormous wealth. Andrew was a shrewd businessman: At the time of his death, he was the president of the Union Savings Bank and director of another bank plus several profitable cotton mills.

Despite his wealth, Andrew was miserly. Though some of his neighbors' homes had running hot water, the three-story Borden home had just two cold-water taps, and there was no water available above the first floor. The Bordens' only latrine was in the cellar, so they generally used chamber pots that were either dumped onto the lawn behind the house or emptied into the cellar toilet. And, although most wealthy people used gas lighting, the Bordens lit their house with inexpensive kerosene lamps.

Worst of all, for many years, Andrew was an undertaker who offered some of the lowest prices in town. He worked on the bodies in the basement of the Borden home, and allegedly, he bent the knees of the deceased—and in some cases, cut off their feet—to fit the bodies into smaller, less expensive coffins in order to increase his business. So, despite the brutality of Andrew's murder, it seems few people mourned his loss. The question wasn't why he was killed, but who did it.

LIZZIE VS. WILLIAM

In 1997, when psychic Jane Doherty visited the murder site, she uncovered several clues about the Lizzie Borden case. Doherty felt that the real murderer was someone named "Willie." There is no real evidence to support this claim, but some say Andrew had an illegitimate son named William, who may have spent time as an inmate in an insane asylum. His constant companion was reportedly his hatchet, which he talked to as though it were a friend. Also, at least one witness reportedly saw William at the Borden house on the day of the murders. William was supposedly there to challenge Andrew about his new will.

Was William the killer? A few years after the murders, William took poison and then hung himself in the woods. Near his swinging body, he'd reportedly left his hatchet on the ground. So with William dead and Lizzie already acquitted, the Borden murder case was put to rest.

LIZZIE'S FORBIDDEN ROMANCE

One of the most curious explanations for the murder involves the Bordens' servant Bridget Sullivan. Her participation has always raised questions. Like the other members of the Borden household, Bridget had suffered from apparent food poisoning the night before the murders. She claimed to have been ill in the backyard of the Borden home. During the time Abby was being murdered, Bridget was apparently washing windows in the back of the house. Later, when Andrew was killed, Bridget was resting in her room upstairs. Why didn't she hear two people being butchered?

According to some theories, Lizzie and Bridget had been romantically involved. In this version of the story, their relationship was discovered shortly before the murders. Around this same time, Andrew was reportedly rewriting his will. His wife was now "Mrs. Borden," to Lizzie, not "Mother," as Lizzie had called her stepmother for many years. The reason for the estrangement was never clear.

Lizzie also had a strange relationship with her father and

had given him her high school ring, as though he were her sweetheart. He wore the ring on his pinky finger and was buried with it.

Just a day before the murders, Lizzie had been attempting to purchase prussic acid—a deadly poison—and the family came down with "food poisoning" that night. Some speculate that Bridget was Lizzie's accomplice in the murders and helped clean up the blood afterward.

This theory was bolstered when, a few years after the murders, Lizzie became involved with actress Nance O'Neil. For two years, Lizzie and the statuesque actress were inseparable. This prompted Emma Borden, Lizzie's sister, to move out of their home.

At the time, the rift between the sisters sparked rumors that either Lizzie or Emma might reveal more about the other's role in the 1892 murders. However, neither of them said anything new about the killings.

WHODUNIT?

Most people believe that Lizzie was the killer. She was the only one accused of the crime, with good reason. Lizzie appeared to be the only one in the house at the time, other than Bridget. She showed no signs of grief when the murders were discovered. During questioning, Lizzie changed her story several times. The evidence was entirely circumstantial, but it was compelling enough to go to trial.

Ultimately, the jury accepted her attorney's closing argument, that the murders were "morally and physically impossible for this young woman defendant." In other words, Lizzie had to be innocent because she was petite and well bred. In 19th-century New England, that seemed like a logical and persuasive defense. Lizzie went free, and

no one else was charged with the crimes.

But Lizzie wasn't the only one with motive, means, and opportunity. The most likely suspects were family members, working alone or with other relatives. Only a few had solid alibis, and—like Lizzie—many changed their stories during police questioning. But there was never enough evidence to officially accuse anyone other than Lizzie.

So whether or not Lizzie Borden "took an ax" and killed her parents, she's the one best remembered for the crime.

LIZZIE BORDEN BED & BREAKFAST

The Borden house has been sold several times over the years, but today it is a bed- and-breakfast—the main draw, of course, being the building's macabre history. The Victorian residence has been restored to reflect the details of the Borden home at the time of the murders, including the couch on which Andrew lay, his skull hideously smashed.

As a guest, you can stay in one of six rooms, even the one in which Abby was murdered. Then, after a good night's sleep, you'll be treated to a breakfast reminiscent of the one the Bordens had on their final morning in 1892. That is, if you got to sleep at all. (They say the place is haunted.)

As with all good morbid attractions, the proprietors at the Lizzie Borden B&B don't take themselves too seriously. Before you leave, you can stop by the gift shop and pick up a pair of hatchet earrings, an "I Survived the Night at the Lizzie Borden Bed & Breakfast" t-shirt, or an ax-wielding Lizzie Borden bobble-head doll.

6 OF HISTORY'S COLDEST CASES

They were gruesome crimes that shocked us with their brutality. But as time passed, we heard less and less about them until we forgot about the crime, not even realizing that the perpetrator remained among us. Yet the files remain open, and the families of the victims live on in a state of semi-paralysis. Here are some of the world's most famous cold cases.

1. The Zodiac Killer: The Zodiac Killer was responsible for several murders in the San Francisco area in the 1960s and 1970s. His victims were shot, stabbed, and bludgeoned to death. After the first few kills, he began sending letters to the local press in which he taunted police and made public threats, such as planning to blow up a school bus. In a letter sent to the San Francisco Chronicle two days after the murder of cabbie Paul Stine in October 1969, the killer, who called himself "The Zodiac," included in the package pieces of Stine's blood-soaked shirt. In the letters, which continued until 1978, he claimed a cumulative tally of 37 murders.

2. Swedish Prime Minister Olof Palme: On February 28, 1986, Swedish Prime Minister Olof Palme was gunned down on a Stockholm street as he and his wife strolled home from the movies unprotected around midnight. The prime minister was fatally shot in the back. His wife was seriously wounded but survived. In 1988, a petty thief and drug addict named Christer Petterson was convicted of the murder because he was picked out of a lineup by Palme's widow. The conviction was later over-turned on appeal when doubts were raised as to the reli-ability of Mrs. Palme's evidence. Despite many theories, the assassin remains at large.

3. Bob Crane: In 1978, Bob Crane, star of TV's *Hogan's Heroes*, was clubbed to death in his apartment. Crane shared a close friendship with John Carpenter, a pioneer in the development of video technology. The two shared an affinity for debauchery and sexual excesses, which were recorded on videotape. But by late 1978, Crane was tiring of Carpenter's dependence on him and had let him know that the friendship was over.

The following day, June 29, 1978, Crane was bludgeoned to death with a camera tripod in his Scottsdale, Arizona, apartment. Suspicion immediately fell on Carpenter, and a small spattering of blood was found in Carpenter's rental car, but police were unable to connect it to the crime. Examiners also found a tiny piece of human tissue in the car. Sixteen years after the killing, Carpenter finally went to trial, but he was acquitted due to lack of evidence.

4. Tupac Shakur: On September 7, 1996, successful rap artist Tupac Shakur was shot four times in a drive-by shooting in Las Vegas. He died six days later. Two years prior to that, Shakur had been shot five times in the lobby of a Manhattan recording studio the day before he was found guilty of sexual assault. He survived that attack, only to spend the next 11 months in jail. The 1994 shooting was a major catalyst for an East Coast- West Coast feud that would envelop the hip-hop industry and culminate in the deaths of both Shakur and Notorious B.I.G. (Christopher Wallace).

On the night of the fatal shooting, Shakur attended the Mike Tyson-Bruce Seldon fight at the MGM Grand in Las

Vegas. After, Shakur and his entourage got into a scuffle with a gang member. Shakur then headed for a night-club, but he never made it. No one was ever arrested for the killing.

5. Jimmy Hoffa: In 1975, labor leader Jimmy Hoffa disappeared on his way to a Detroit-area restaurant. Hoffa was the president of the Teamsters Union during the 1950s and 1960s. In 1964, he went to jail for bribing a grand juror investigating corruption in the union. In 1971, he was released on the condition that he not participate in any further union activity. Hoffa was preparing a legal challenge to that injunction when he disappeared on July 30, 1975. He was last seen in the parking lot of the Machus Red Fox Restaurant.

Hoffa had strong connections to the Mafia, and several mobsters have claimed that he met a grisly end on their say so. Although his body has never been found, authorities officially declared him dead on July 30, 1982. As recently as November 2006, the FBI dug up farmland in Michigan hoping to turn up a corpse. So far, no luck.

6. JonBenét Ramsey: In the early hours of December 26, 1996, Patsy Ramsey reported that her six-year-old daughter, JonBenét, had been abducted from her Boulder, Colorado, home. Police rushed to the Ramsey home where, hours later, John Ramsey found his little girl dead in the basement. She had been battered, sexually assaulted, and strangled.

Police found several tantalizing bits of evidence—a number of footprints, a rope that did not belong on the premises, marks on the body that suggested the use of a stun gun, and DNA samples on the girl's body. The ransom note was also suspicious. Police found that it was written with a pen and pad of paper belonging to the Ramseys. The amount demanded, $118,000, was a surprisingly small amount, considering that John Ramsey was worth more than $6 million. It is also interesting to note that Mr. Ramsey had just received a year-end bonus of $118,117.50.

A number of suspects were considered, but one by one they were cleared. Finally, the police zeroed in on the parents. For years, the Ramseys were put under intense pressure by authorities and the public alike to confess to the murder. However, a grand jury investigation ended with no indictments. In 2003, a judge ruled that an intruder had killed JonBenét. Then, in August 2006, John Mark Karr confessed, claiming that he was with the girl when she died. However, Karr's DNA did not match that found on JonBenét. He was not charged, and the case remains unsolved.

THOMAS INCE: A BOATING EXCURSION TURNS DEADLY

Film mogul Thomas Ince joins other Hollywood notables for a weekend celebration in 1924 and ends up dead. Was it natural causes or one of the biggest cover-ups in Hollywood history?

The movie industry has been rocked by scandal throughout its history, but few incidents have matched the controversy and secrecy surrounding the death of Thomas Ince, a high-profile producer and director of many successful silent films. During the 1910s, he set up his own studio in California where he built a sprawling complex of small homes, sweeping mansions, and other buildings that were used as sets for his movies. Known as Inceville, the studio covered several thousand acres, and it was there that Ince perfected the idea of the studio system—a factory-style setup that used a division of labor amongst large teams of costumers, carpenters, electricians, and other film professionals who moved from project to project as needed. This system, which allowed for the mass production of movies with the producer in creative and financial control, would later be adopted by all major Hollywood film companies.

Down on his luck by the 1920s, Ince still had many influential friends and associates. In November 1924, newspaper magnate William Randolph Hearst offered to host a weekend birthday celebration for the struggling producer aboard his luxury yacht the *Oneida*. Several Hollywood luminaries attended, including Charlie Chaplin and Marion Davies, as well Louella Parsons, then a junior writer for one of Hearst's East Coast newspapers. But at the end of the cruise, Ince was carried off the ship on a medical gurney and rushed home, where he died two days later. A hastily scribbled death certificate blamed heart failure.

THE RUMORS FLY

Almost immediately, the rumor mill churned out shocking and sordid versions of the incident, which were very different from the official line. A Chaplin employee, who was waiting at the docks when the boat returned, reportedly claimed that Ince was suffering from a gunshot wound to the head when he was taken off the *Oneida*. Could he have been the victim of a careless accident at the hands of a partying Hollywood celeb? Perhaps, but film industry insiders knew of complex and passionate relationships among those on board, and a convoluted and bizarre scenario soon emerged and has persisted to this day. As it turns out, Davies was Hearst's longtime mistress, despite being almost 34 years his junior. She was also a close friend of the notorious womanizer Chaplin. Many speculate that Hearst, enraged over the attention that Chaplin was paying to the young ingenue, set out to kill him but shot the hapless Ince by mistake.

Certain events after Ince's death helped the rumors gain traction. Ince's body was cremated, so no autopsy could be performed. And his grieving widow was whisked off to Europe for several months courtesy of Hearst—conveniently away from the reach of the American press. Louella Parsons was also elevated within the Hearst organization, gaining a lifetime contract and the plum assignment as his number-one celebrity gossip columnist, which she parlayed into a notoriously self-serving enterprise. Conspiracy theorists believe that she wrangled the deal with Hearst to buy her silence about the true cause of Ince's death.

LINGERING MYSTERY

Was Ince the victim of an errant gunshot and subsequent cover-up? If anyone in 1920s California had the power to hush witnesses and bend officials to his will in order to get away with murder, it was the super rich and powerful Hearst. But no clear evidence of foul play has emerged after all these decades. Still, the story has persisted and even served as the subject for *The Cat's Meow*, a 2002 film directed by Peter Bogdanovich, which starred Kirsten Dunst as Davies and Cary Elwes as the doomed Ince.

WILLIAM DESMOND TAYLOR

The murder of actor/director William Desmond Taylor was like something out of an Agatha Christie novel, complete with a handsome, debonair victim and multiple suspects, each with a motive. But unlike Christie's novels, in which the murderer was always unmasked, Taylor's death remains unsolved nearly 90 years later.

On the evening of February 1, 1922, Taylor was shot in the back by an unknown assailant; his body was discovered the next morning by a servant, Henry Peavey. News of Taylor's demise spread quickly, and several individuals, including officials from Paramount Studios, where Taylor was employed, raced to the dead man's home to clear it of anything incriminating, such as illegal liquor, evidence of drug use, illicit correspondence, and signs of sexual indiscretion. However, no one called the police until later in the morning.

NUMEROUS SUSPECTS

Soon an eclectic array of potential suspects came to light, including Taylor's criminally inclined former butler, Edward F. Sands, who had gone missing before the murder; popular movie comedienne Mabel Normand, whom Taylor had entertained the evening of his death; actress Mary Miles Minter, who had a passionate crush on the handsome director who was 28 years her senior; and Charlotte Shelby, Minter's mother, who often wielded a gun to protect her daughter's tarnished honor.

Taylor's murder was the last thing Hollywood needed at the time, coming as it did on the heels of rape allegations against popular film comedian Fatty Arbuckle. Scandals brought undue attention on Hollywood, and the Arbuckle story had taken its toll. Officials at Paramount tried to keep a lid on the Taylor story, but the tabloid press had a field day. A variety of personal foibles were made public in the weeks that followed, and both Normand and Minter saw their careers come to a screeching halt as a result. Taylor's own indiscretions were also revealed, such as the fact that he kept a special souvenir, usually lingerie, from every woman he bedded.

LITTLE EVIDENCE

Police interviewed many of Taylor's friends and colleagues, including all potential suspects. However, there was no evidence to incriminate anyone specifically, and no one was formally charged.

Investigators and amateur sleuths pursued the case for years. Sands was long a prime suspect, based on his criminal past and his estrangement from the victim. But it was later revealed that on the day of the murder, Sands had signed in for work at a lumberyard in Oakland, California—some 400 miles away—and thus could not have committed the crime. Coming in second was Shelby, whose temper and threats were legendary. Shelby's own acting career had fizzled out early, and all of her hopes for stardom were pinned on her daughter. She threatened many men who tried to woo Mary.

In the mid-1990s, another possible suspect surfaced—a long-forgotten silent-film actress named Margaret Gibson. According to Bruce Long, author of *William Desmond Taylor: A Dossier*, Gibson confessed to a friend on her deathbed in 1964 that years before she had killed a man named William Desmond Taylor. However, the woman to whom Gibson cleared her conscience didn't know who Taylor was and thought nothing more about it.

THE MYSTERY CONTINUES

Could Margaret Gibson (aka Pat Lewis) be Taylor's murderer? She had acted with Taylor in Hollywood in the early 1910s, and she may even have been one of his many sexual conquests. She also had a criminal past, including charges of blackmail, drug use, and prostitution, so it's entirely conceivable that she was a member of a group trying to extort money from the director, a popular theory among investigators. But according to an earlier book, *A Cast of Killers* by Sidney D. Kirkpatrick, veteran Hollywood director King Vidor had investigated the murder as material for a film script and through his research believed Shelby was the murderer. But out of respect for Minter, he never did anything about it.

Ultimately, however, we may never know for certain who killed William Desmond Taylor, or why. The case has long grown cold, and anyone with specific knowledge of the murder is likely dead. Unlike a Hollywood thriller, in which the killer is revealed at the end, Taylor's death is a macabre puzzle that likely will never be solved.

OHIO'S GREATEST UNSOLVED MYSTERY

From 1935 until 1938, a brutal madman roamed the Flats of Cleveland. The killer—known as the Mad Butcher of Kingsbury Run—is believed to have murdered 12 men and women. Despite a massive manhunt, the murderer was never apprehended.

In 1935, the Depression had hit Cleveland hard, leaving large numbers of people homeless. Shantytowns sprang up on the eastern side of the city in Kingsbury Run—a popular place for transients—near the Erie and Nickel Plate railroads.

It is unclear who the Butcher's first victim was. Recent research suggests it may have been an unidentified woman found floating in Lake Erie—in pieces—on September 5, 1934; she would be known as Jane Doe I but dubbed by some as the Lady of the Lake. The first official victim was found in the Jackass Hill area of Kingsbury Run on September 23, 1935. The unidentified body, labeled John Doe, had been dead for almost a month. A mere 30 feet away from the body was another victim, Edward Andrassy. Unlike John Doe, Andrassy had only been dead for days, indicating that the spot was a dumping ground. Police began staking out the area.

After a few months passed without another body, police thought the worst was over. Then on January 26, 1936, the partial remains of a new victim, a woman, were found in downtown Cleveland. On February 7, more remains were found at a separate location, and the deceased was identified as Florence Genevieve Polillo. Despite similarities among the three murders, authorities had yet to connect them—serial killers were highly uncommon at the time.

TATTOO MAN, ELIOT NESS, AND MORE VICTIMS

On June 5, two young boys passing through Kingsbury Run discovered a severed head. The rest of the body was found near the Nickel Plate railroad police station. Despite six distinctive tattoos on the man's body (thus the nickname "Tattoo Man"), he was never identified and became John Doe II.

At this point, Cleveland's newly appointed director of public safety, Eliot Ness, was officially briefed on the case. While Ness and his men hunted down leads, the headless body of another unidentified male was found west of Cleveland on July 22, 1936. It appeared that the man, John Doe III, had been murdered several months earlier. On September 10, the headless body of a sixth victim, John Doe IV, was found in Kingsbury Run.

Ness officially started spearheading the investigation. Determined to bring the killer to justice, Ness's staff fanned out across the city, even going undercover in the Kingsbury Run area. As 1936 drew to a close, no suspects had been named nor new victims discovered. City residents believed that Ness's team had run the killer off. But future events would prove that the killer was back... with a vengeance.

THE BODY COUNT CLIMBS

A woman's mutilated torso washed up on the beach at 156th Street on February 23, 1937. The rest would wash ashore two months later. (Strangely, the body washed up in the same location as the Lady of the Lake had three years earlier.)

On June 6, 1937, teenager Russell Lauyer found the decomposed body of a woman inside of a burlap sack under the Lorain-Carnegie Bridge in Cleveland. With the body was a newspaper from June of the previous year, suggesting a timeline for the murder. An investigation indicated the body might belong to one Rose Wallace; this was never confirmed, and the victim is sometimes referred to as Jane Doe II. Pieces of another man's body (the ninth victim) began washing ashore on July 6, just below Kingsbury Run. Cleveland newspapers were having a field day with the case that the "great" Eliot Ness couldn't solve. This fueled Ness, and he promised justice.

BURNING OF KINGSBURY RUN

The next nine months were quiet, and the public began to relax. When a woman's severed leg was found in the Cuyahoga River on April 8, 1938, however, people debated its connection to the Butcher. But the rest of Jane Doe III was soon found inside two burlap sacks floating in the river (sans head, of course).

On August 16, 1938, the last two confirmed victims of the Butcher were found together at the East 9th Street Lakeshore Dump. Jane Doe IV had apparently been dead for four to six months prior to discovery, while John Doe VI may have been dead for almost nine months.

Something snapped inside Eliot Ness. On the night of August 18, Ness and dozens of police officials raided the shantytowns in the Flats, ending up in Kingsbury Run. Along the way, they interrogated or arrested anyone they came across, and Ness ordered the shanties burned to the ground. There would be no more confirmed victims of the Mad Butcher of Kingsbury Run.

WHO WAS THE MAD BUTCHER?

There were two prime suspects in the case, though no one was ever charged. The first was Dr. Francis Sweeney, a surgeon with the knowledge many believed necessary to mutilate the victims the way the killer did. (He was also a cousin of Congressman Martin L. Sweeney, a known political opponent of Ness.)

In August 1938, Dr. Sweeney was interrogated by Ness, two other men, and the inventor of the polygraph machine, Dr. Royal Grossman. By all accounts, Sweeney failed the polygraph test (several times), and Ness believed he had his man, but he was released due to lack of evidence.

Two days after the interrogation, on August 25, 1938, Sweeney checked himself into the Sandusky Veterans Hospital. He remained institutionalized at various facilities until his death in 1965. Because Sweeney voluntarily checked himself in, he could have left whenever he desired.

The other suspect was Frank Dolezal, who was arrested by private investigators on July 5, 1939, as a suspect in the murder of Florence Polillo, with whom he had lived for a time. While in custody, Dolezal confessed to killing Polillo, although some believe the confession was forced. Either way, Dolezal died under mysterious circumstances while incarcerated at the Cuyahoga County Jail before he could be charged.

As for Eliot Ness, some believe his inability to bring the Butcher to trial weighed on him for the rest of his life. Ness went to his grave without getting a conviction. To this day, the case remains open.

CHAPTER 3
EVASIVE CREATURES

THE DEVIL IS ALIVE AND WELL... AND LIVING IN NEW JERSEY

The Pine Barrens consist of more than a million acres of forested land in central and southern New Jersey. So named because the area's sandy, acidic soil is bad for growing crops, it has proven a fertile home for an amazing collection of trees and plants. Of course, if the stories are true, the area is also home to a bizarre winged creature known as the Jersey Devil.

BIRTH OF THE DEVIL

There are many legends concerning the origin of the Jersey Devil. The most popular involves the Leeds family, who came to America from Europe in the 1730s and settled in the southern area of the Pine Barrens. The Leeds family quickly grew by leaps and bounds, and before long, their house was filled with a dozen children. Needless to say, when Mother Leeds found out she was pregnant with child number 13, she was less than enthusiastic. In fact, she supposedly yelled out that she was done having children and that this child "could be the devil" for all she cared. Apparently someone was listening, for when the 13th child was born, it allegedly resembled a devil, complete with wings, a tail, and cloven hooves. Once born, the child devoured its 12 siblings and its parents, then promptly disappeared into the Pine Barrens, where it still lives to this day.

THE FIRST SIGHTINGS

One of the first, and most intriguing, sightings of the Jersey Devil took place in the early 1800s when Commodore Stephen Decatur saw a bizarre creature flying overhead as he was test-firing cannons at the Hanover Iron Works. Perhaps wishing to test the accuracy of the cannons, Decatur took aim and fired upon the creature overhead, striking one of its wings. To the amazement of Decatur and the other onlookers, the creature didn't seem to care that it had just been shot by a cannonball and casually flew away.

From the mid-1800s until the early 1900s, there were numerous sightings of the Jersey Devil throughout the Pine Barrens and beyond. Those who actually witnessed it described it as being everything from short and hairy to tall and cranelike. But there was one thing everyone agreed upon—whatever the creature was, it was not of this earth.

1909: THE YEAR OF THE DEVIL

At the beginning of 1909, thousands of people encountered the beast in the span of a week. On Saturday, January 16, a winged creature believed to be the Jersey Devil was spotted flying over the town of Woodbury, New Jersey. The following day, residents of Bristol, Pennsylvania, also reported seeing something strange flying in the sky. Later the same day, bizarre tracks were discovered in the snow. Then on Monday, January 18, residents of Burlington, New Jersey, and neighboring towns were perplexed by the strange tracks in the snow on their rooftops. They had no clue as to who or what left them. All the while, reports kept coming in of something strange flying overhead with a head resembling a horse and hooves for feet.

In the early morning hours of January 19, Nelson Evans and his wife got up close and personal with the Jersey Devil outside their Gloucester, New Jersey, home. At approximately 2:30 a.m., a creature standing more than eight feet tall with a "head like a collie dog and a face like a horse" peered into the Evanses' window. Although they were petrified, Nelson mustered up the courage to open the window and yell at the creature. Startled, the creature turned, made a barking sound, and then flew off. Later that day, two Gloucester hunters claimed they had tracked strange footprints in the snow for nearly 20 miles. As they followed the tracks, they noticed that whatever this creature was, it not only had the ability to fly or leap over large areas, but it could also squeeze underneath fences and through small spaces.

By Wednesday, January 20, local towns were forming posses intent on tracking down the Jersey Devil. They were all unsuccessful, although they did have several sightings of the winged creature flying toward neighboring towns. Then on Thursday, things really got out of hand. The day began with the Devil reportedly attacking a trolley car in Haddon Heights. It was also during this time that local farmers reported finding some of their livestock missing or dead. And in Camden, New Jersey, a dog was attacked by the Jersey Devil and only managed to survive when its owner chased the beast away.

By Friday, the Devil had been spotted all over New Jersey and in parts of Pennsylvania. During that time, the creature had been shot at (and was supposedly struck by several bullets) and was even hosed down by a local fire department, but this didn't seem to phase the beast at all.

SIGHTINGS CONTINUE

As news of the Jersey Devil spread, it seemed that the entire nation descended upon New Jersey in an attempt to catch a glimpse of or, better yet, capture, the creature. But despite all the searching and even a $10,000 reward for the beast's capture, it was never caught.

It appears that after its very busy week in 1909, the Jersey Devil decided to lay low. In fact, though sightings did continue through the years, they were few and far between. Because of this, people started to believe that the Jersey Devil was a harbinger of doom and would only be sighted when something bad was going to happen. Of course, this did not stop hundreds of people from wandering through the Pine Barrens in search of the beast. But no matter how hard people looked, not a single photograph or piece of video exists of the creature. Part of the reason certainly has to be that the Pine Barrens has remained virtually the same vast and undeveloped area, making it the perfect place for a devil to hide. So for now, the Pine Barrens is keeping its secret.

MONSTER ON THE CHESAPEAKE

Chesapeake Bay, a 200-mile intrusion of the Atlantic Ocean into Virginia and Maryland, is 12 miles wide at its mouth, allowing plenty of room for strange saltwater creatures to slither on in. Encounters with giant, serpentine beasts up and down the Eastern seaboard were reported during the 1800s, but sightings of Chessie, a huge, snakelike creature with a football-shape head and flippers began to escalate in the 1960s. Former CIA employee Donald Kyker and some neighbors saw not one, but four unidentified water creatures swimming near shore in 1978.

In 1980, the creature was spotted just off Love Point, sparking a media frenzy. Two years later, Maryland resident Robert Frew was entertaining dinner guests with his wife, Karen, when the whole party noticed a giant water creature about 200 yards from shore swimming toward a group of people frolicking nearby in the surf. They watched the creature, which they estimated to be about 30 feet in length, as it dove underneath the unsuspecting humans, emerged on the other side, and swam away.

Frew recorded several minutes of the creature's antics, and the Smithsonian Museum of Natural History reviewed his film. Although they could not identify the animal, they did concede that it was animate.

THE CHESSIE CHALLENGE

Some believe Chessie is a manatee, but they usually swim in much warmer waters and are only about ten feet long. Also, the fact that Chessie is often seen with several "humps" breaking the water behind its head leads other investigators to conclude that it could be either a giant sea snake or a large seal.

One Maryland resident has compiled a list of 78 different sightings over the years. And a tour boat operator offers sea-monster tours in hopes of repeating the events of 1980 when 25 passengers on several charter boats all spotted Chessie cavorting in the waves.

BIGFOOT: THE KING OF ALL MONSTERS

Let's face it—if you had to pick one monster that stands head (and feet) above all others, it would be Bigfoot. Not only is it the stuff of legends, but its likeness has also been used to promote everything from pizza to beef jerky. Bigfoot has had amusement park rides and monster trucks named after it and was even slated to be one of the mascots for the 2010 Winter Olympics in Vancouver, British Columbia.

EARLY SIGHTINGS

Folktales from Native American tribes throughout the Northwest, the area that Bigfoot traditionally calls home, are filled with references to giant, apelike creatures roaming the woods. They described the beast as between seven and ten feet tall and covered in brown or dark hair. (Sasquatch, a common term used for the big-footed beast, is actually an anglicization of a Native American term for a giant supernatural creature.)

Walking on two legs, there was something humanlike about Sasquatch's appearance, although its facial features more closely resembled that of an ape, and it had almost no neck. With looks like that, it's not surprising that Native American folklore often described the creature as cannibalistic, supernatural, and dangerous. Other tales, however, said Sasquatch appeared to be frightened of humans and mostly kept to itself.

It wasn't until the 1900s, when more and more woodlands were being devoured in the name of progress, that Sasquatch sightings started to increase. It was believed that, though generally docile, the beast did have a mean streak when feeling threatened. In July 1924, Fred Beck and several others were mining in a mountainous area of Washington State. One evening, the group spotted and shot at what appeared to be an apelike creature. After fleeing to their cabin, the group was startled when several more hairy giants began banging on the walls, windows, and doors. For several hours, the creatures pummeled the cabin and threw large rocks at it before disappearing shortly before dawn. After several such encounters in the same general vicinity, the area was renamed Ape Canyon.

MY, WHAT BIG FEET YOU HAVE!

In August 1958, Jerry Crew, a bulldozer operator, showed up for work at a wooded site in Bluff Creek, California. Walking up to his bulldozer, which had been left there overnight, Crew found giant footprints in the dirt. At first, they appeared to be the naked footprints of a man, but with one major difference—these feet were huge! After the tracks appeared on several occasions, Crew took a cast of one of them and brought it to *The Humboldt Times* in Eureka, California. The following day, the newspaper ran a front-page story, complete with photos of the footprint and a name for the creature: Bigfoot. The story and photographs hit the Associated Press, and the name stuck.

Even so, the event is still rife with controversy. Skeptics claim that it was Ray Wallace, not Bigfoot, who made the tracks as a practical joke on his brother Wilbur, who was Crew's supervisor. Apparently the joke backfired when Crew arrived at the site first and saw the prints before Wilbur. However, Ray Wallace never admitted to faking the tracks or having anything to do with perpetrating a hoax.

VIDEO EVIDENCE?

In 1967, in response to numerous Bigfoot sightings in northern California, Roger Patterson rented a 16mm video camera in hopes of filming the elusive creature. Patterson and his friend, Robert Gimlin, spent several days on horseback traveling though the Six Rivers National Forest without coming across as much as a footprint.

Then, on October 20, the pair rounded a bend and noticed something dark and hairy crouched near the water. When the creature stood up on two legs and presented itself in all its hairy, seven-foot glory, that's when Patterson said he knew for sure he was looking at Bigfoot. Unfortunately, Patterson's horse saw the creature, too, and suddenly reared up. Because of this, it took Patterson several precious seconds to get off the horse and remove the video camera from his saddlebag. Once he did that, he ran toward the creature, filming as he went.

As the creature walked away, Patterson continued filming until his tape ran out. He quickly changed his film, and then both men retrieved their frightened horses and attempted to follow Bigfoot further before eventually losing sight of it.

When they arrived back in town, Patterson reviewed the film. Even though it was less than a minute long and extremely shaky in spots, the film appeared to show Bigfoot running away while occasionally looking toward the camera. For most Bigfoot enthusiasts, the Patterson–Gimlin film stands as the Holy Grail of Bigfoot sightings—physical proof captured on video. Skeptics, however, alleged that Patterson and Gimlin faked the entire incident and filmed a man in an expensive monkey suit. Nevertheless, more than 40 years after the event occurred, the Patterson–Gimlin film is still one of the most talked about pieces of Bigfoot evidence, mainly because neither man ever admitted to a hoax and the fact that no one has been able to figure out how they faked it.

GONE SASQUATCHING

The fact that some people doubt the existence of Bigfoot hasn't stopped thousands of people from heading into the woods to try to find one. Even today, the hairy creature makes brief appearances here and there. Of course, sites like YouTube have given rise to dozens of "authentic" videos of Bigfoot, some of which are quite comical.

Still, every once in a while, a video that deserves a second look pops up. For example, in 2005, ferry operator Bobby Clarke filmed almost three minutes of video of a Bigfoot-like creature on the banks of the Nelson River in Manitoba. And in late 2007, photos taken by a hunter in Pennsylvania's Allegheny National Forest were being analyzed.

SPOTTING SASQUATCH

Throughout the world, it's called Alma, Yeti, Sasquatch, the Abominable Snowman, Wildman, and Bigfoot. Whatever the name, people agree that it's tall, hairy, doesn't smell good, and has a habit of showing up in locations around the globe—especially in North America.

JASPER, ALBERTA, CANADA (1811)

This was the first known Bigfoot evidence found in North America. An explorer named David Thompson found 14-inch footprints in the snow, each toe topped by a short claw. He and his party didn't follow the tracks, fearing their guns would be useless against such a large animal. In his journal he wrote that he couldn't bring himself to believe such a creature existed.

TOBA INLET, BRITISH COLUMBIA, CANADA (1924)

In 1957, prospector Albert Ostman was finally able to come forward about a chilling event that happened to him more than 30 years prior. While camping at the head of Toba Inlet near Vancouver Island, Ostman was snatched up, still in his sleeping bag, and taken to a small valley where several Bigfoot were living. Held captive for several days, Ostman was only able to escape when one of the larger creatures tried to eat his snuff and chaos ensued.

WANOGA BUTTE, OREGON (1957)

After a long, uneventful morning hunting, Gary Joanis and Jim Newall were ecstatic when Joanis felled a deer with a single shot. But when a hairy creature "not less than nine feet tall" emerged from the woods, threw the deer over its shoulder, and lumbered off, the two men were left speechless.

MONROE, MICHIGAN (1965)

On August 13, Christine Van Acker and her mother were driving when a large, hairy creature came out of the nearby woods. Frightened by the creature, the mother lost control of the car and grazed the beast. The car stalled and while the mother struggled to start it, the creature put its arm through the window, struck Christine in the face and slammed her mother's head against the car door, leaving both women with black eyes—photos of which were widely circulated in the press.

SPEARFISH, SOUTH DAKOTA (1977)

Betty Johnson and her three daughters saw two Bigfoot in a cornfield. The larger of the two was eight-feet tall; the other, slightly smaller. They both appeared to be eating corn and making a whistling sound.

PARIS TOWNSHIP, OHIO (1978)

Herbert and Evelyn Cayton reported that a seven-foot-tall, 300-pound, fur-covered creature appeared at their house so frequently that their daughter thought it was a pet.

JACKSON, WYOMING (1980)

On June 17, Glenn Towner and Robert Goodrich went into the woods on Snow King Mountain to check out a lean-to built by a friend of theirs. After hearing moaning and growling, the pair was chased out of the woods by a 12-foot-tall creature covered in hair. The creature followed them back to civilization, where it was last spotted standing briefly beneath a streetlight before vanishing back into the woods.

CRESCENT CITY, CALIFORNIA (1995)

A TV crew was driving in their RV, filming the scenery in Jedediah Smith Redwoods State Park, when an eight-foot-tall hairy giant crossed their path and was caught on tape.

COTTON ISLAND, LOUISIANA (2000)

Bigfoot surprised lumberjacks Earl Whitstine and Carl Dubois while they were clearing timber. The hairy figure returned a few days later, leaving behind footprints and hair samples.

SELMA, OREGON (2000)

While hiking with his family near the Oregon Caves National Monument on July 1, psychologist Matthew Johnson smelled a strange musky odor. Hearing odd grunting noises coming from behind some trees, Johnson went to investigate and saw something very tall and hairy walking away. When asked to describe it, Johnson said that it could be "nothing else but a Sasquatch."

GRANTON, WISCONSIN (2000)

As James Hughes was delivering newspapers early one morning, he saw a shaggy figure, about eight feet tall, carrying a goat. However, sheriffs called to the scene couldn't find any footprints or missing goats.

MT. ST. HELENS, WASHINGTON (2002)

Jerry Kelso made his wife and two-year-old child wait in the car, while he chased what he thought was a man in a gorilla suit. When he was about 100 feet away, he realized that it wasn't a gorilla suit and that the seven-foot-tall creature was carrying a club.

CRANBROOK, BRITISH COLUMBIA, CANADA (2007)

Snowplow driver Gord Johnson drove by a large, hairy figure with a "conical head" walking along a snowy road.

WEREWOLVES IN WISCONSIN?

Do you believe in werewolves? If you head out to southeastern Wisconsin, you might just meet one face-to-fang.

MEETING THE BEAST

The first recorded sighting of the Beast came in 1936, long before it even had a name. Security guard Mark Schackelman was walking the grounds of a convent near Jefferson shortly before midnight when he saw a strange creature digging on top of a Native American burial mound. As Schackelman got closer, the creature ran off into the darkness. The scene repeated itself the following night, but this time, the creature stood up on its hind legs, growled at the shocked security guard, and simply walked away.

Encounters like this have continued through the years. Most people describe the creature as six to eight feet tall. It gets around on all fours but can also walk on two feet. Its entire body is covered with fur (similar to Bigfoot), but this Beast also has clawed hands, the head of a wolf, and bright yellow eyes. With a description like that, it's easy to see why some people believe that the creature is a werewolf. But several people have seen the Beast in broad daylight.

THE BEAST GETS A NAME

In the early 1990s, an outbreak of Beast sightings in southeastern Wisconsin—specifically, along an isolated stretch of Bray Road, just outside the town of Elkhorn—led a local reporter to dub the creature The Beast of Bray Road.

Today, the Beast continues to linger around southeastern Wisconsin, but it's seldom seen on Bray Road anymore. It was, however, spotted in Madison in 2004. So if you're ever driving through the area, keep an eye out for what might be lurking around the bend.

RED EYES OVER POINT PLEASANT: THE MYSTERIOUS MOTHMAN

In 1942, the U.S. government took control of several thousand acres of land just north of Point Pleasant, West Virginia. The purpose was to build a secret facility capable of creating and storing TNT that could be used during World War II. For the next three years, the facility cranked out massive amounts of TNT, shipping it out or storing it in one of the numerous concrete "igloo" structures that dotted the area. In 1945, the facility was shut down and eventually abandoned, but it was here that an enigmatic flying creature with glowing red eyes made its home years later.

"RED EYES ON THE RIGHT"

On the evening of November 15, 1966, Linda and Roger Scarberry were out driving with another couple, Mary and Steve Mallette. As they drove, they decided to take a detour that took them past the abandoned TNT factory.

As they neared the gate of the old factory, they noticed two red lights up ahead. When Roger stopped the car, the couples were horrified  to find that the red lights appeared to be two glowing red eyes. What's more, those eyes belonged to a creature standing more than seven feet tall with giant wings folded behind it. That was all Roger needed to see before he hit the gas pedal and sped off. In response, the creature calmly unfolded its wings and flew toward the car. Incredibly, even though Roger raced along at speeds close to 100 miles per hour, the red-eyed creature was able to keep up with them without much effort.

Upon reaching Point Pleasant, the two couples ran from their car to the Mason County Courthouse and alerted Deputy Millard Halstead of their terrifying encounter. Halstead couldn't be sure exactly what the two couples had seen, but whatever it was, it had clearly frightened them. In an attempt to calm them down, Halstead agreed to accompany them to the TNT factory. As his patrol car neared the entrance, the police radio suddenly emitted a strange, whining noise. Other than that, despite a thorough search of the area, nothing out of the ordinary was found.

MORE ENCOUNTERS

Needless to say, once word got around Point Pleasant that a giant winged creature with glowing red eyes was roaming around the area, everyone had to see it for themselves. The creature didn't disappoint. Dubbed Mothman by the local press, the creature was spotted flying overhead, hiding, and even lurking on front porches. In fact, in the last few weeks of November, dozens of witnesses encountered the winged beast. But Mothman wasn't the only game in town. It seems that around the same time that he showed up, local residents started noticing strange lights in the evening sky, some of which hovered silently over the abandoned TNT factory. Of course, this led some to believe that Mothman and the UFOs were somehow connected. One such person was Mary Hyre of *The Athens Messenger*, who had been reporting on the strange activities in Point Pleasant since they started. Perhaps that's why she became the first target.

BEWARE THE MEN IN BLACK

One day, while Mary Hyre was at work, several strange men visited her office and began asking questions about the lights in the sky. Normally, she didn't mind talking to people about the UFO sightings and Mothman. But there was something peculiar about these guys. For instance, they all dressed exactly the same: black suits, black ties, black hats, and dark sunglasses. They also spoke in a strange monotone and seemed confused by ordinary objects such as ballpoint pens. As the men left, Hyre wondered whether they had been from another planet. Either way, she had an up-close-and-personal encounter with the legendary Men in Black.

Mary Hyre was not the only person to have a run-in with the Men in Black. As the summer of 1967 rolled around, dozens of people were interrogated by them. In most cases, the men showed up unannounced at the homes of people who had recently witnessed a Mothman or UFO sighting. For the most part, the men simply wanted to know what the witnesses had seen. But sometimes, the men went to great lengths to convince the witnesses that they were mistaken and had not seen anything out of the ordinary. Other times, the men threatened witnesses. Each time the Men in Black left a witness's house, they drove away in a black, unmarked sedan. Despite numerous attempts to determine who these men were and where they came from, their identity remained a secret. And all the while, the Mothman sightings continued throughout Point Pleasant and the surrounding area.

THE SILVER BRIDGE TRAGEDY

Erected in 1928, the Silver Bridge was a gorgeous chain suspension bridge that spanned the Ohio River, connecting Point Pleasant with Ohio. On December 15, 1967, the bridge was busy with holiday shoppers bustling back and forth between West Virginia and Ohio. As the day wore on, more and more cars started filling the bridge until shortly before 5:00 p.m., when traffic on the bridge came to a standstill. For several minutes, none of the cars budged. Suddenly, there was a loud popping noise and then the unthinkable happened: The Silver Bridge collapsed, sending dozens of cars and their passengers into the freezing water below.

Over the next few days, local authorities and residents searched the river hoping to find survivors, but in the end, 46 people lost their lives in the bridge collapse. A thorough investigation determined that a manufacturing flaw in one of the bridge's supporting bars caused the collapse. But there are others who claim that in the days and weeks leading up to the collapse, they saw Mothman and even the Men in Black around, on, and even under the bridge. Further witnesses state that while most of Point Pleasant was watching the Silver Bridge collapse, bright lights and strange objects were flying out of the area and disappearing into the winter sky. Perhaps that had nothing to do with the collapse of the Silver Bridge, but the Mothman has not been seen since…or has he?

MOTHMAN LIVES!

There are reports that the Mothman is still alive and well and has moved on to other areas of the United States. There are even those who claim that he was spotted flying near the Twin Towers on September 11, 2001, leading to speculation that Mothman is a portent of doom and only appears when disasters are imminent. Some believe Mothman was a visitor from another planet who returned home shortly after the Silver Bridge fell. Still others think the creature was the result of the toxic chemicals eventually discovered in the area near the TNT factory. And then there are skeptics who say that the initial sighting was nothing more than a giant sand crane and that mass hysteria took care of the rest. Whichever theory you choose to believe, the Mothman Lives website compiles all sightings of the creature from the 1960s to the present.

THE CHAMPION OF AMERICAN LAKE MONSTERS

In 1609, French explorer Samuel de Champlain was astonished to see a thick, eight- to ten-foot-tall creature in the waters between present-day Vermont and New York. His subsequent report set in motion the legend of Champ, the "monster" in Lake Champlain.

EERIE ENCOUNTERS

Even before Champlain's visit, Champ was known to Native Americans as Chaousarou. Over time, Champ has become one of North America's most famous lake monsters. News stories of its existence were frequent enough that in 1873, showman P. T. Barnum offered $50,000 for the creature, dead or alive. That same year, Champ almost sank a steamboat, and in the 1880s, a number of people, including a sheriff, glimpsed it splashing playfully offshore. It is generally described as dark in color (olive green, gray, or brown) with a serpentlike body.

Sightings have continued into modern times, and witnesses have compiled some film evidence that is difficult to ignore. In 1977, a woman named Sandra Mansi photographed a long-necked creature poking its head out of the water near St. Albans, Vermont, close to the Canadian border. She estimated the animal was 10 to 15 feet long and told an investigator that its skin looked "slimy" and similar to that of an eel. Mansi presented her photo and story at a 1981 conference held at Lake Champlain. Although she had misplaced the negative by then, subsequent analyses of the photo have generally failed to find any evidence that it was manipulated.

In September 2002, a researcher named Dennis Hall, who headed a lake monster investigation group known as Champ Quest, videotaped what looked like three creatures undulating through the water near Ferrisburgh, Vermont. Hall claimed that he saw unidentifiable animals in Lake Champlain on 19 separate occasions.

In 2006, two fishermen captured digital video footage of what appeared to be parts of a very large animal swimming in the lake. The images were thoroughly examined under the direction of ABC News technicians, and though the creature on the video could not be proved to be Champ, the team could find nothing to disprove it, either.

CHAMP OR CHUMP?

As the sixth-largest freshwater lake in the United States (and stretching about six miles into Quebec, Canada), Lake Champlain provides ample habitat and nourishment for a good-size water cryptid, or unknown animal. The lake plunges as deep as 400 feet in spots and covers 490 square miles.

Skeptics offer the usual explanations for Champ sightings: large sturgeons, floating logs or water plants, otters, or an optical illusion caused by sunlight and shadow. Others think Champ could be a remnant of a species of primitive whale called a zeuglodon or an ancient marine reptile known as a plesiosaur, both believed by biologists to be long extinct. But until uncontestable images of the creature's entire body are produced, this argument will undoubtedly continue.

Champ does claim one rare, official nod to the probability of its existence: Legislation by both the states of New York and Vermont proclaim that Champ is a protected—though unknown—species and make it illegal to harm the creature in any way.

MONSTERS ACROSS AMERICA

Dracula, Frankenstein, the Wolf Man—these are the monsters who strike fear into the hearts of children—the same ones that parents chase away and tell their kids there's no such thing as monsters. But are they wrong?

DOVER DEMON

For two days in 1977, the town of Dover, Massachusetts, was under attack from a bizarre creature that seemed to be from another world. The first encounter with the beast—nicknamed the Dover Demon—occurred on the evening of April 21. Bill Bartlett was out for a drive with some friends when they saw something strange climbing on a stone wall. The creature appeared to be only about three feet tall but had a giant, oversize head with large, orange eyes. The rest of the body was tan and hairless with long, thin arms and legs.

Several hours later, the same creature was spotted by 15-year-old John Baxter, who watched it scurry up a hillside. The following day, a couple reported seeing the Demon, too. When authorities asked for a description, the couple's matched the ones given by the other witnesses except for one difference: The creature the couple encountered appeared to have glowing green eyes. Despite repeated attempts to locate it, the creature was never seen again.

MOMO

In the early 1970s, reports came flooding in of a strange creature roaming the woods near the small town of Louisiana, Missouri. Standing nearly seven feet tall, Momo (short for Missouri Monster) was completely covered in black fur with glowing orange eyes. The first major report came in July 1971 when Joan Mills and Mary Ryan claimed to have been harassed by a "half ape, half man" creature that made bizarre noises at them as they passed it on Highway 79. Even though the creature didn't make physical contact with them, both women believed it would have harmed them had it been given the chance. That seemed to be confirmed the following year when, on July 11, 1972, brothers Terry and Wally Harrison spotted a giant, hairy beast carrying a dead dog. The boys screamed, alerting family members, who caught a glimpse of the creature before it disappeared into the woods. Sightings continued for a couple of weeks, but Momo hasn't been seen since.

LAWNDALE THUNDERBIRD

If you're ever in Lawndale, Illinois, keep an eye out for giant birds lest they sneak up on you and whisk you away. That's what almost happened in 1977 when Lawndale residents noticed two large black birds with white-banded necks and 10- to 12-foot wingspans flying overhead. The birds, though enormous, seemed harmless enough. That is, until they swooped down and one of them reportedly tried to take off with ten- year-old Marlon Lowe while he played in his yard. The boy was not seriously injured, but the thunderbird did manage to lift the terrified boy several feet off the ground and carry him for nearly 40 feet before dropping him. Over the next few weeks, the birds were seen flying over various houses and fields in nearby towns, but, thankfully, they did not attack anyone else. And though they appear to have left Lawndale for good, reports of thunderbird sightings continue across the United States. The most recent one was on September 25, 2001, in South Greensburg, Pennsylvania.

OHIO BRIDGE TROLLS

In May 1955, a man driving along the Miami River near Loveland, Ohio, came across a frightening sight. Huddled under a darkened bridge were several bald-headed creatures, each three to four feet tall. Spellbound, the man pulled over and watched the creatures, which he said had webbed hands and feet. Though they made no sound, the man said the creatures appeared to be communicating with each other and did not notice him watching them. However, when one of the creatures held up a wand or rod that began emitting showers of sparks, the man quickly left. He drove straight to the local police station, which dispatched a car to the bridge. A search of the area turned up nothing, and, to this day, there have been no more reported sightings of these strange creatures.

MARYLAND'S GOATMAN

Think goats are cute and fuzzy little creatures? If so, a trip through Prince George's County in Maryland just might change your mind. Since the 1950s, people have reported horrifying encounters with a creature known only as the Goatman. From afar, many claim to have mistaken the Goatman for a human being. But as he draws nearer, his cloven feet become visible, as do the horns growing out of his head. If that's not enough to make you turn and run, reports as recent as 2006 state that the Goatman now carries an ax with him.

GATORMEN

The swamplands of Florida are filled with alligators, but most of them don't have human faces. Since the 1700s, tales of strange half-man, half-alligator creatures have circulated throughout the area. Gatormen are described as having the face, neck, chest, and arms of a man and the midsection, back legs, and tail of an alligator. Unlike most other monsters and strange beasts, Gatormen reportedly prefer to travel and hunt in packs and even appear to have their own verbal language. What's more, recent sightings have them traveling outside the state of Florida and taking up residence in the swamplands of Louisiana and swimming around a remote Texas swamp in 2001.

SKUNK APE

Since the 1960s, a creature has been spotted in the Florida Everglades that many call Bigfoot's stinky cousin: the skunk ape. The beast is said to closely resemble Bigfoot with one minor difference—it smells like rotten eggs. In late 2000, Sarasota police received an anonymous letter from a woman who complained that an escaped animal was roaming near her home at night. Included with the letter were two close-up photographs of the creature—a large beast that resembled an orangutan standing behind some palmetto leaves, baring its teeth.

LIZARD MAN

At around 2:00 a.m. on June 29, 1988, Christopher Davis got a flat tire on a back road near the Scape Ore Swamp in South Carolina. Just as the teen finished changing the tire, he was suddenly attacked by a seven-foot-tall creature with scaly green skin and glowing red eyes. Davis was able to get back into his car and drive away but not before the Lizard Man managed to climb onto the roof and claw at it, trying to get inside. As he drove, Davis could see the creature had three claws on each of its "hands." Eventually, the creature fell from the car and Davis was able to escape. A search of the scene later that day turned up nothing. Despite numerous subsequent sightings, the creature has yet to be apprehended.

DEVIL MONKEYS

Far and away, some of the strangest creatures said to be roaming the countryside are the Devil Monkeys. Take an adult kangaroo, stick a monkey or baboon head on top, and you've got yourself a Devil Monkey. By most accounts, these creatures can cover hundreds of feet in just a few quick hops. They're nothing to tangle with, either. Although Devil Monkeys have traditionally stuck to attacking livestock and the occasional family pet, some reports have them attempting to claw their way into people's homes. Originally spotted in Virginia in the 1950s, Devil Monkeys have now been spotted all across the United States.

MYTHICAL CREATURES

From the time man first began telling tales around the campfire, every human culture has described creatures with characteristics quite different from run-of-the-mill animals. The legends of horses and snakes with wings, behemoths with horns in odd places, or other conglomerations live on to tease us with questions of their existence.

DRAGONS: REAL SCORCHERS

One of the oldest and most universal mythical creatures is the dragon. Huge, winged lizards or serpents with greenish scales and flaming breath are found in tales from ancient China to medieval Europe.

In China, the dragon originally represented the rising sun, happiness, and fertility. Sumerians included dragons in their religious art as early as 4000 BC. The ancient Greeks called their dragon Draco and pictured it as a massive, winged snake emitting light and squeezing victims to death in its coils.

In the British Isles, dragons were associated with the legendary King Arthur and St. George, and though it is generally accepted that dragons do not exist, some think ancient man's glimpses of giant sea snakes may have inspired dragon myths.

UNICORNS: CREATURES THAT MAKE A POINT

Variations of the unicorn, a horse with a single, long horn growing out of its forehead, appear in myths worldwide. It is possible that a similar, actual creature may have appeared at one time to inspire these myths. In the 1800s, a French woman grew a single, ten-inch horn from her forehead. A wax casting of the horn is preserved in Philadelphia's Mütter Museum. More recently, in 2003, a 95-year-old woman began growing a similar horn. By May 2007, it was five inches long. These are called cutaneous (skin-related) horns and, if possible in humans, could also logically occur in other large mammals. Unicorns are usually portrayed as snow white, gentle, noble creatures—each with a very long, twisted horn that comes to a sharp point.

PEGASUS: CLOUD GALLOPER

Greek legend has it that when Poseidon, god of the sea, got together with Medusa, the gorgon with the snake-infested hair, their offspring was Pegasus, a great white horse with wings. Pegasus became the mount of the hero Bellerophon, and together they slew the bizarre Chimera (a fire-breathing monster with the head of a lion, body of a goat, and tail of a snake). Pride in the great deed made Bellerophon think he could ride Pegasus to Mt. Olympus, home of the gods, so he sprang away for the heavens. But the mortal Bellerophon was thrown back to Earth by Zeus, who kept the winged horse for himself. There is a constellation named for Pegasus.

CYCLOPS: KEEPING AN EYE OUT

They were not pretty, according to Greek legend. The small group of grotesque, one-eyed giants called Cyclopes (in the plural) was warlike and given to eating human flesh. Their one skill was an astonishing talent for creating weapons for the gods, such as swords and arrows. Could such people ever have existed? Humans inflicted with an endocrine disorder known as gigantism have been known to reach a height of eight feet, and very rarely humans may also be born with a birth defect that gives them a single eye, so perhaps this monster has roots in a long-forgotten, actual human being.

HAVING A LOT OF FAUN

Very similar to goat-man creatures called satyrs but not at all related to baby deer (fawns), fauns looked like men from the navel up, except for the goat horns sprouting from their temples. They also bounded about on goat legs and hooves. Fathered by the Greek god Faunus, fauns protected the natural world, especially fields and woods. They were also similar in appearance to Pan, Greek god of nature, who gave us the word panic for the fright he could inspire by blowing on his magical conch shell. Mr. Tumnus from C. S. Lewis's *The Lion, the Witch, and the Wardrobe* was a faun.

CENTAURS: WHEN HORSE AND RIDER ARE TRULY ONE

A skilled rider will often appear as one with his or her galloping steed, so it isn't hard to see how ancient Greeks may have envisioned a creature that was human-like from the trunk up but with the legs and body of a stallion—it makes for truly seamless horsemanship. Centaurs were meat-eating revelers who loved to drink, according to Greek legend, except for one gentle man-horse named Chiron known for his wisdom and teaching abilities. Chiron lives on as the centaur constellation Sagittarius, and centaurs are still seen on the coats of arms of many old European families.

TROLLS: MAMMOTH MOUNTAIN MEN

Although the descriptions of these ugly, manlike beings vary from country to country, trolls originated in Scandinavian lands, where they were said to be gigantic, grotesque humanoids who lived in the hills or mountains, mined ore, and became wondrous metal smiths. Trolls could turn to stone if caught in the sun, and Norway's ancient rock pillars are said to be evidence of this belief. But perhaps legends of trolls are based on a few individuals with a disorder that would not have been understood in ancient times. A rare hormonal disorder called gigantism causes excessive growth of the long bones, and, thus, greatly increased height.

GRIFFINS: IN THE CAT-BIRD SEAT?

Depictions of these folk monsters can be found in artwork from ancient Egypt and other cradles of civilization as early as 3300 BC. Mainly a lion-eagle combo, griffins featured a lion's body and an eagle's wings, head, and legs. But they also sported big ears and fierce, ruby-colored eyes. Griffins often guarded rich treasure troves and viciously defended their turf with their sharp beaks and talons. They have survived in modern fantasy fiction, including Lewis Carroll's *Alice's Adventures in Wonderland*.

FAIRIES: NOT ALWAYS TINKERBELL

Fairies, also known as wood nymphs, sprites, pixies, and many other names in cultures around the world, are usually thought of as attractive little spirit beings, proportioned like humans and charmingly dressed in wildflowers and acorns. In modern times, they are often depicted as sweet little beings with translucent wings. But in medieval times, the *fée* or fay, as they were called in Old French or English, could be naughty or nice.

One Irish tradition maintains that fairies often stole babies, substituting an old, wrinkled fairy or even a bundled log in place of the infant. Some European folk traditions believed fairies were descended from an old, superior race of humanoid creatures, and others thought they were fallen angels that had landed in woods or meadows. Shakespeare's play, *A Midsummer Night's Dream*, with its royal fairies Oberon and Titania, helped popularize the notion of fairies as small, magical people living in their own kingdom among humans. And folk belief worldwide still insists that these little people must be treated respectfully and given offerings and gifts to keep them from pulling nasty tricks on their human neighbors.

MYTHICAL SEA MONSTERS

Seafarers of old were respectful and wary of the strange creatures that lurked below the surface. The reflection of sunlight upon water, overwhelming homesickness, or too much drink caused many sailors to see monsters.

KRAKEN

The kraken was one of the most horrifying creatures a sailor could encounter. It was believed to be a many-armed monster—described by one 14th-century writer as resembling an uprooted tree—that would wrap itself around a ship, pull down its masts, and drag it to the bottom of the ocean. The creature was so large that it could be mistaken for a small island. Early whalers often saw tentacle and suction marks on the bodies of sperm whales, which served to cement the kraken's terrifying reputation. Modern sailors recognize the kraken as a giant squid, which is an enormous, octopuslike mollusk. The giant squid has a long, torpedo-shaped body, even longer tentacles, and eyes that are more than 18 inches in diameter. They grow to lengths of 60 feet (sometimes more) and weigh nearly a ton. Although not often seen by humans, these deep-sea dwellers have been known to attack whales and tanker ships.

SEA SERPENTS

Some of the most famous sea monsters, such as Loch Ness's "Nessie," are commonly believed to be of the serpent persuasion. Whether in saltwater or freshwater, a sea serpent looks similar to a snake or dragon and usually has several "humps." Although cryptozoologists hold out hope that these creatures are some sort of surviving dinosaur, that's not likely the case. It is theorized that freshwater sea serpents, such as Lake Tahoe's "Tahoe Tessie," are actually snakes—perhaps giant anacondas— that escaped from a passing boat. Naysayers point out that tropical anacondas don't do well in mountainous, high-altitude winters.

Ocean-dwelling sea serpents are easier to explain. For centuries, witnesses have mistaken basking sharks, rows of diving dolphins, clumps of sargassum seaweed, seals, and even undulating waves for the head and humps of a sea serpent. Perhaps the most common explanation, however, is the oarfish, which resembles an eel and grows to 26 feet in length (and has been reported at three times that size).

MERMAIDS

Mermaids—aquatic creatures with a woman's torso and the tail of a fish—have been spotted in oceans and lakes around the world since 1000 BC. In the past few centuries, several supposedly authentic mermaid specimens have been displayed, but all of them have proved to be hoaxes. These include P. T. Barnum's famous "Feejee Mermaid"; taxidermic creations consisting of sewn parts of monkeys and fish; and "Jenny Hannivers," which are carcasses of rays, skates, or cuttlefish carved and varnished to resemble a winged sea monster with a hideous human head. The name is likely an anglicization of jeune de Anvers, or "girl of Antwerp," in reference to the Belgian port where 16th- and 17th-century sailors made and sold these popular souvenirs.

Seals and sea otters, both known for their playful interaction with humans, have likely been mistaken for mermaids. The legendary selkie—a mythical seal that sheds its skin on land and resumes it while in the sea—derives from mermaid folklore. The dugong and manatee are both cowlike, sea-dwelling mammals that nurse their young above water. In fact, the word manatee comes from the Carib word for breasts, which could explain why mermaids are said to be naked from the waist up. Of course, it's also possible that mermaid stories were made up by hapless sailors or fishermen who needed an excuse for spying on skinny-dipping women.

CHAPTER 4
UNCHARTED, UNEXPLORED, & UNKNOWN

WHO WANTS TO BE A BILLIONAIRE?

According to legend, more than $2 billion in gold may be hidden on Oak Island in Mahone Bay, about 45 minutes from Halifax, Nova Scotia. For more than 200 years, treasure hunters have scoured the island, looking for the bounty, but the pirates who buried the treasure hid it well…and left booby traps, too.

FOLKLORE LEADS TO FACT

Since 1720, people have claimed that pirate treasure was buried on Oak Island. Then, in the fall of 1795, young Daniel McGinnis went hunting on the island and found evidence that those stories might be true. But he found something rather odd: An oak tree had been used with a hoist to lift something very heavy. When McGinnis dug at that spot, he found loose sand indicating a pit about 12 feet in diameter.

He returned the next day with two friends

and some digging tools. When the boys had dug ten feet down, they encountered a wooden platform—beneath it was more dirt. Ten feet further down, they reached another wooden platform with more dirt beneath it. At that point, the boys had to give up. They needed better tools and engineering expertise to continue their search.

They didn't get the help they needed, but one thing was certain: Something important had been buried on Oak Island. Soon, more people visited the island hoping to strike it rich.

AN ENCOURAGING MESSAGE

In the early 1800s, a Nova Scotia company began excavating the pit. The slow process took many years, and every ten feet, they found another wooden platform and sometimes layers of charcoal, putty, or coconut fiber.

About 90 feet down, the treasure hunters found an oily stone about three feet wide. It bore a coded inscription that read, "Forty feet below, £2 million lie buried." (Gold worth £2 million in 1795 would be worth approximately $2 billion today.)

However, as they dug past that 90-foot level, water began rushing into the hole. A few days later, the pit was almost full of seawater. No matter how much the team bailed, the water maintained its new level, so the company dug a second shaft, parallel to the first and 110 feet deep. But when they dug across to the original tunnel, water quickly filled the new shaft as well. The team abandoned the project, but others were eager to try their luck.

MORE DIGGING, MORE ENCOURAGEMENT, MORE WATER

Since then, several companies have excavated deeper in the original shaft. Most treasure hunters—including a team organized by Franklin D. Roosevelt—have found additional proof that something valuable is buried there. For example, at 126 feet—nearly "forty feet below" the 90-foot marker—engineers found oak and iron. Farther down, they also reached a large cement chamber, from which they brought up a tiny piece of parchment, which encouraged them to dig deeper.

A narrow shaft dug in 1971 allowed researchers to use special cameras to study the pit. The team thought they saw several chests, some tools, and a disembodied hand floating in the water, but the shaft collapsed before they could explore further. Since then, flooding has continued to hamper research efforts, and at least six people have been killed in their quests to find buried treasure. Nevertheless, the digging continues.

As of late 2007, the 1971 shaft had been redug to a depth of 181 feet. It offers the greatest promise for success. But just in case, investors and engineers plan to continue digging.

A VACATION WORTH A FORTUNE?

But the digging isn't limited to professionals. Oak Island has become a unique vacation spot for people who like adventure and the chance to go home with a fortune. Canadian law says any treasure hunter can keep 90 percent of his or her findings.

Some vacationers dig at nearby islands, believing that the Oak Island site may be an elaborate, 18th-century red herring. There are more than 100 other lovely islands in Mahone Bay. Perhaps the treasure is actually buried on one of them?

THE MYSTERY OF MONTAUK

Montauk, a beach community at the eastern tip of Long Island in New York state, has been designated the Miami Beach of the mid-Atlantic. Conspiracy theorists, however, tell another tale. Has the U.S. government been hiding a secret at the former Camp Hero military base there?

In the late 1950s, Montauk was not the paradise-style resort it is today. It was an isolated seaside community boasting a lighthouse commissioned by George Washington in 1792, an abandoned military base called Camp Hero, and a huge radar tower. This tower, still standing, is the last semiautomatic ground environment radar tower still in existence and features an antenna called AN/FPS-35. During its time of Air Force use, the AN/FPS-35 was capable of detecting airborne objects at a distance of more than 200 miles. One of its uses was detecting potential Soviet long-distance bombers, as the Cold War was in full swing. According to conspiracy theorists, however, the antenna and Camp Hero itself had a few other tricks lurking around the premises, namely human mind control and electro-magnetic field-manipulation.

VANISHING ACT

On October 24, 1943, the USS *Eldridge* was allegedly made invisible to human sight for a brief moment as it sat in a naval shipyard in Philadelphia. The event, which has never been factually substantiated but has been sworn as true by eyewitnesses and other believers for decades, is said to have been part of a U.S. military endeavor called the Philadelphia Experiment, or Project Rainbow. Studies in electromagnetic radiation had evidenced that manipulating energy fields and bending light around objects in certain ways could render them invisible. Since the benefits to the armed forces would be incredible, the navy supposedly forged ahead with the first experiment.

There are many offshoots to the conspiracy theory surrounding the alleged event. The crew onboard the USS *Eldridge* at the time in question are said to have suffered various mental illnesses, physical ailments, and, most notably, schizophrenia, which has been medically linked to exposure to electromagnetic radiation. Some of them supposedly disappeared along with the ship and relocated through teleportation to the naval base in Norfolk, Virginia, for a moment. Despite severely conflicting eyewitness reports and the navy's assertion that the *Eldridge* wasn't even in Philadelphia that day, many websites, books, a video game, and a 1984 science fiction film detail the event.

But what does this have to do with Montauk right now?

WHAT'S IN THE BASEMENT?

Camp Hero was closed as an official U.S. Army base in November 1957, although the Air Force continued to use the radar facilities. After the Air Force left in 1980, the surrounding grounds were ultimately turned into a state park, which opened to the public in September 2002. Yet the camp's vast underground facility remains under tight government jurisdiction, and the AN/FPS-35 radar tower still stands. Many say there is a government lab on-site that continues the alleged teleportation, magnetic field manipulation, and mind-control experiments that originated with Project Rainbow. One reason for this belief is that two of the sailors onboard the *Eldridge* on October 24, 1943—Al Bielek and Duncan Cameron—claimed to have jumped from the ship while it was in "hyperspace" between Philadelphia and Norfolk, and landed at Camp Hero, severely disoriented.

Though Project Rainbow was branded a hoax, an urban legend continues to surround its legacy, which is commonly known as the Montauk Project. Theorists cite experiments in electromagnetic radiation designed to produce mass schizophrenia over time and reduce a populace's resistance to governmental control, which, they believe, would explain the continual presence of the antenna. According to these suspicions, a large number of orphans, loners, and homeless people are subjected to testing in Camp Hero's basement; most supposedly die as a result. Interestingly, some conspiracy theorists believe that one outcropping of the experiments is the emergence and rapid popularity of the cell phone, which uses and produces electromagnetic and radio waves. Who knew that easier communication was really an evil government plot to turn people into mindless robots?

THE LOST CITY OF ATLANTIS

Ever since Plato first mentioned the ancient civilization of Atlantis in his dialogues Timaeus and Critias, academic analysts have debated the existence of the lost continent. Was the prophetic philosopher fabricating a tale or indicating valuable information?

According to Plato, the ancient civilization of Atlantis was a colossal naval power that conquered many parts of Western Europe and Africa more than 9,000 years before the time of Solon, or approximately 9500 BC. After a failed attempt to invade Athens, the entire continent collapsed into the ocean "in a single day and night of misfortune." Since Plato never bothered to divulge the manner of demise, historians have been left to argue over the authenticity of the alleged Atlantis. The skeptical side of the ledger contends that Plato was using his cre-

ative leverage to force his readers to both examine and question the limitations and logistics of greed, government, and power. Simply put, Plato's message was that power corupts and the price paid is high.

IDENTIFYING ATLANTIS

In 2004, Robert Sarmast, a U.S. author, architect, and explorer, announced that he had found circumstantial evidence of the existence of Atlantis 1,500 meters deep in the Mediterranean Sea between Cyprus and Syria. But Sarmast also admitted that he "cannot yet provide tangible proof in the form of bricks and mortar, as the artifacts are still buried under several meters of sediment. We hope that future expeditions will be able to uncover the sediment and bring back physical proof." Until that happens, however, the evidence of Atlantis is inconclusive.

THREE SIDES TO EVERY STORY

Few geographical locations on Earth have been discussed and debated more than the three-sided chunk of ocean between the Atlantic coast of Florida and the regions of San Juan, Puerto Rico, and Bermuda known as the Bermuda Triangle.

Over the centuries, hundreds of ships and dozens of airplanes have mysteriously disappeared while floating in or flying through the region commonly called the Bermuda Triangle. Myth mongers propose that alien
forces are responsible for these dissipations. Because little or no wreckage from the vanished vessels has ever been recovered, paranormal pirating has also been cited as the culprit. Other theorists suggest that leftover technology from the lost continent of Atlantis—mainly an underwater rock formation known as the Bimini Road (situated just off the island of Bimini in the Bahamas)—exerts a supernatural power that grabs unsuspecting intruders and drags them to the depths.

A DEADLY ADJECTIVE

Although the theory of the Triangle had been mentioned in publications as early as 1950, it wasn't until the '60s that the region was anointed with its three-sided appellation. Columnist Vincent Gaddis wrote an article in the February 1964 edition of *Argosy* magazine that discussed the various mysterious disappearances that had occurred over the years and designated the area where myth and mystery mixed as the "Deadly Bermuda Triangle." The use of the adjective deadly perpetrated the possibility that UFOs, alien anarchists, supernatural beings, and metaphysical monsters reigned over the region. The mystery of Flight 19, which involved the disappearance of five planes in 1945, was first noted in newspaper articles that appeared in 1950, but its fame was secured when the flight and its fate were fictitiously featured in Steven Spielberg's 1977 alien opus, *Close Encounters of the Third Kind*. In Hollywood's view, the pilots and their planes were plucked from the sky by friendly aliens and later returned safely to terra firma by their abductors.

In 1975, historian, pilot, and researcher Lawrence David Kusche published one of the first definitive studies that dismissed many of the Triangle theories. In his book *The Bermuda Triangle Mystery—Solved*, he concluded that the Triangle was a "manufactured mystery," the result of bad research and reporting and, occasionally, deliberately falsified facts. Before weighing anchor on Kuche's conclusions, however, consider that one of his next major publications was a tome about exotic popcorn recipes.

EXPLAINING ODD OCCURRENCES

Other pragmatists have insisted that a combination of natural forces—a double whammy of waves and rain that create the perfect storm—is most likely the cause for these maritime misfortunes. Other possible "answers" to the mysteries include rogue waves (such as the one that capsized the Ocean Ranger oil rig off the coast of Newfoundland in 1982), hurricanes, underwater earthquakes, and human error. The Coast Guard receives almost 20 distress calls every day from amateur sailors attempting to navigate the slippery sides of the Triangle. Modern-day piracy—usually among those involved in drug smuggling—has been mentioned as a probable cause for odd occurrences, as have unusual magnetic anomalies that screw up compass readings. Other possible explanations include the Gulf Stream's uncertain current, the high volume of sea and air traffic in the region, and even methane hydrates (gas bubbles) that produce "mud volcanoes" capable of sucking a ship into the depths.

THE FOUNTAIN OF YOUTH

It's been an obsession of explorers for centuries, but no one has been able to find the magic elixir.

Spanish explorer Juan Ponce de León was supposedly searching for the fabled fountain of youth when he discovered Florida. However, it wasn't until after his death in 1521 that he became linked with the fountain.

The first published reference associating Ponce de León with the fountain of youth was the *Historia General y Natural de las Indias*, by Gonzalo Fernandez de Oviedo in 1535. The author cited the explorer's search for a fountain of restorative water to cure his impotence, but the veracity of this account is questionable since Ponce de León had children at the time of his 1513 voyage and didn't even mention the fountain in his travel notes.

Moreover, the fountain of youth legend predates Ponce de León. In Arabic versions of the *Alexander Romance*, a collection of myths about Alexander the Great, the Macedonian king and his troops cross a desert and come to a fountain in which they bathe to regain strength and youth. This story was translated to French in the 13th century and was well known among Europeans.

If a fountain of youth actually exists, no one has found it in it in any of its supposed locations, which are most typically cited as Florida, the Bahamas, or the Bay of Honduras. It may turn out, however, that a fountain of youth exists in science. David Sinclair, a Harvard University professor and the founder of Sirtris Pharmaceuticals, discovered in 2003 that the molecule resveratrol could extend the lifespan of worms and fruit flies. In 2006, Italian researchers prolonged the life of the fish *Nothobranchius furzeri* with resveratrol.

Drugs that are based on this research could be on shelves soon, though initially they will be designed only to aid diabetics. It's not quite eternal life—it's basically just extended fitness. But that's more than Ponce de León found.

THE SECRET OF THE STONES

Part of the enduring charm of Stonehenge—that curious structure of rocks located in Wiltshire County, southern England—is that it continues to defy explanation, baffling experts throughout the centuries.

Though no one can definitively say who erected this massive monument, when and why they built it, and how they did so without the aid of modern machinery, there are no shortage of theories. So let's hear from the experts:

Archaeologists: Speculate that the site first took shape about 5,000 years ago, with the first stones being laid in 3000 BC. The monument was finally completed in 1500 BC, perhaps serving as a memorial to fallen warriors, as the burial mounds that surround the site might indicate.

Geologists: Claim that 80 of the 4-ton rocks at Stonehenge, known as bluestones, were quarried from the Prescelly Mountains in Wales—240 miles away—and then transported by sled and barge to their current location.

Astronomers: Observe that builders placed the rocks in concentric circles, thus creating a massive solar observatory through which early man could predict the arrival of eclipses and follow the passage of the seasons. On the longest day of the year, the rising sun appears directly behind one of the main stones, the so-called Heel Stone.

Historians: Think that the stones form the walls of an ancient temple—a place for people to worship the heavens. In later times, it was used by Druids to celebrate their pagan festivals.

Conspiracy theorists: Believe Stonehenge was placed there by a UFO.

THE NAZCA LINES—PICTURES AIMED AT AN EYE IN THE SKY?

Ancient works of art etched into a desert floor in South America have inspired wild theories about who created them and why. Did space aliens leave them on long-ago visits? Decades of scientific research reject the popular notion, showing that the lines were the work of mere Earthlings.

Flying above the rocky plains northwest of Nazca, Peru, in 1927, aviator Toribio Mejía Xesspe was surprised to see gigantic eyes looking up at him. Then the pilot noticed that the orbs stared out of a bulbous head upon a cartoonish line drawing of a man, etched over hundreds of square feet of the landscape below.

The huge drawing—later called Owl Man for its staring eyes—turned out to be just one of scores of huge, 2,000-year-old images scratched into the earth over almost 200 square miles of the parched Peruvian landscape.

There is a 360-foot-long monkey with a whimsically spiraled tail, along with a 150-foot- long spider, and a 935-foot pelican. Other figures range from hummingbird to killer whale. Unless the viewer knows what to look for, they're almost invisible from ground level. There are also geometric shapes and straight lines that stretch for miles across the stony ground.

THE THEORY OF ANCIENT ASTRONAUTS

The drawings have been dated to a period between 200 BC and AD 600. Obviously, there were no airplanes from which to view them back then. So why were they made? And for whose benefit?

In his 1968 book *Chariots of the Gods?*, Swiss author Erich Von Däniken popularized the idea that the drawings and lines were landing signals and runways for starships that visited southern Peru long before the modern era. In his interpretation, the Owl Man is instead an astronaut in a helmet. Von Däniken's theory caught on among UFO enthusiasts. Many science-fiction novels and films make reference to this desert in Peru's Pampa Colorado region as a site with special significance to space travelers.

COMING DOWN TO EARTH

Examined up close, the drawings consist of cleared paths—areas where someone removed reddish surface rocks to expose the soft soil beneath. In the stable desert climate—averaging less than an inch of rain per year—the paths have survived through many centuries largely intact.

Scientists believe the Nazca culture—a civilization that came before the Incas—drew the lines. The style of the artwork is similar to that featured on Nazca pottery. German-born researcher Maria Reiche (1903–1998) showed how the Nazca could have laid out the figures using simple surveying tools such as ropes and posts. In the 1980s, American researcher Joe Nickell duplicated one of the drawings, a condor, showing that the Nazca could have rendered parts of the figures "freehand"—that is, without special tools or even scale models. Nickell also demonstrated that despite their great size, the figures can be identified as drawings even from ground level. No alien technology would have been required to make them.

STILL MYSTERIOUS

As for why the Nazca drew giant doodles across the desert, no one is sure. Reiche noted that some of the lines have astronomical relevance. For example, one points to where the sun sets at the winter solstice. Some lines may also have pointed toward underground water sources—crucially important to desert people.

Most scholars think that the marks were part of the Nazca religion. They may have been footpaths followed during ritual processions. And although it's extremely unlikely that they were intended for extraterrestrials, many experts think it likely that the lines were oriented toward Nazca gods—perhaps a monkey god, a spider god, and so on, who could be imagined gazing down from the heavens upon likenesses of themselves.

THE MYSTERY OF EASTER ISLAND

On Easter Sunday in 1722, a Dutch ship landed on a small island 2,300 miles from the coast of South America. Polynesian explorers had preceded them by a thousand years or more, and the Europeans found the descendants of those early visitors still living on the island. They also found a strange collection of almost 900 enormous stone heads, or moai, standing with their backs to the sea, gazing across the island with eyes hewn out of coral. The image of those faces haunts visitors to this day.

ANCESTORS AT THE END OF THE LAND

Easter Island legend tells of the great Chief Hotu Matu'a, the Great Parent, striking out from Polynesia in a canoe, taking his family on a voyage across the trackless ocean in search of a new home. He made landfall on Te-Pito-te-Henua, the End of the Land, sometime between AD 400 and 700. Finding the island well-suited to habitation, his descendants spread out to cover much of the island, living off the natural bounty of the land and sea. With their survival assured, they built *ahu*—ceremonial sites featuring a large stone mound—and on them erected *moai*, which were representations of notable chieftains who led the island over the centuries. The *moai* weren't literal depictions of their ancestors, but rather embodied their spirit, or mana, and conferred blessings and protection on the islanders.

The construction of these *moai* was quite a project. A hereditary class of sculptors oversaw the main quarry, located near one of the volcanic mountains on the island. Groups of people would request a *moai* for their local *ahu*, and the sculptors would go to work, their efforts supported by gifts of food and other goods. Over time, they created 887 of the stone *moai*, averaging just over 13 feet tall and weighing around 14 tons, but ranging from one extreme of just under four feet tall to a behemoth that towered 71 feet. The *moai* were then transported across the island by a mechanism that still remains in doubt, but that may have involved rolling them on the trunks of palm trees felled for that purpose—a technique that was to have terrible repercussions for the islanders.

When Europeans first made landfall on Easter Island, they found an island full of standing *moai*. Fifty-two years later, James Cook reported that many of the statues had been toppled, and by the 1830s none were left standing. What's more, the statues hadn't just been knocked over; many of them had boulders placed at strategic locations, with the intention of decapitating the *moai* when they were pulled down. What happened?

A CULTURE ON THE BRINK

It turns out the original Dutch explorers had encountered a culture on the rebound. At the time of their arrival, they found two or three thousand living on the island, but some estimates put the population as high as fifteen thousand a century before. The story of the islanders' decline is one in which many authors find a cautionary tale: The people simply consumed natural resources to the point where their land could no longer support them. For a millennium, the islanders simply took what they needed: They fished, collected bird eggs, and chopped down trees to pursue their obsession with building moai. By the 1600s, life had changed: The last forests on the island disappeared, and the islanders' traditional food-stuffs disappeared from the archaeological record. Local tradition tells of a time of famine and even rumored cannibalism, and it is from this time that island history reveals the appearance of the spear. Tellingly, the Polynesian words for wood begin to take on a connotation of wealth, a meaning found nowhere else that shares the language. Perhaps worst of all, with their forests gone, the islanders had no material to make the canoes that would have allowed them to leave their island in search of resources. They were trapped, and they turned on one another.

The Europeans found a reduced society that had just emerged from this time of terror. The respite was short-lived, however. The arrival of the foreigners seems to have come at a critical moment in the history of Easter Island. Either coincidentally or spurred on by the strangers, a warrior class seized power across the island, and different groups vied for power. Villages were burned, their resources taken by the victors, and the defeated left to starve. The warfare also led to the toppling of an enemy's moai—whether to capture their mana or simply prevent it from being used against the opposing faction. In the end, none of the moai remained standing.

DOWNFALL AND REBOUND

The troubles of Easter Island weren't limited to self-inflicted chaos. The arrival of the white man also introduced smallpox and syphilis; the islanders, with little natural immunity to the exotic diseases, fared no better than native populations elsewhere. As if that weren't enough, other ships arrived, collecting slaves for work in South America. The internal fighting and external pressure combined to reduce the number of native islanders to little more than a hundred by 1877—the last survivors of a people who once enjoyed a tropical paradise.

Easter Island, or Rapa Nui, was annexed by Chile in 1888. As of 2009, there are 4,781 people living on the island. There are projects underway to raise the fallen *moai*. As of today, approximately 50 have been returned to their former glory.

SANDSTONE GATEWAY TO HEAVEN

For hundreds of years, rumors of the lost city of Angkor spread among Cambodian peasants. On a stifling day in 1860, Henri Mahout and his porters discovered that the ancient city was more than mere legend.

French botanist and explorer Henri Mahout wiped his spectacles as he pushed into the Cambodian jungle clearing. Gasping for breath in the rain forest's thick mists, he gazed down weed-ridden avenues at massive towers and stone temples wreathed with carvings of gods, kings, and battles. The ruins before him were none other than the temples of Angkor Wat.

Although often credited with the discovery of Angkor Wat, Mahout was not the first Westerner to encounter the site. He did, however, bring the "lost" city to the attention of the European public when his travel journals were published in 1868. He wrote: "One of these temples—a rival to that of Solomon, and erected by some ancient Michelangelo—might take an honorable place beside our most beautiful buildings."

Mahout's descriptions of this "new," massive, unexplored Hindu temple sent a jolt of lightning through Western academic circles. Explorers from western Europe combed the jungles of northern Cambodia in an attempt to explain the meaning and origin of the mysterious lost shrine.

THE RISE OF THE KHMER

Scholars first theorized that Angkor Wat and other ancient temples in present-day Cambodia were about 2,000 years old. However, as they began to decipher the Sanskrit inscriptions, they found that the temples had been erected during the 9th through 12th centuries. While Europe languished in the Dark Ages, the Khmer Empire of Indochina was reaching its zenith.

The earliest records of the Khmer people date back to the middle of the 6th century. They migrated from southern China and settled in what is now Cambodia. The early Khmer retained many Indian influences from the West—they were Hindus, and their architecture evolved from Indian methods of building.

In the early 9th century, King Jayavarman II laid claim to an independent kingdom called Kambuja. He established his capital in the Angkor area some 190 miles north of the modern Cambodian capital of Phnom Penh. Jayavarman II also introduced the cult of devaraja, which claimed that the Khmer king was a representative of Shiva, the Hindu god of chaos, destruction, and rebirth. As such, in addition to the temples built to honor the Hindu gods, temples were also constructed to serve as tombs when kings died.

The Khmer built more than 100 stone temples spread out over about 40 miles. The temples were made from laterite (a material similar to clay that forms in tropical climates) and sandstone. The sandstone provided an open canvas for the statues and reliefs celebrating the Hindu gods that decorate the temples.

HOME OF THE GODS

During the first half of the 12th century, Kambuja's King Suryavarman II decided to raise an enormous temple dedicated to the Hindu god Vishnu, a religious monument that would subdue the surrounding jungle and illustrate the power of the Khmer king. His masterpiece—the largest temple complex in the world—would be known to history by its Sanskrit name, Angkor Wat, or "City of Temple."

Pilgrims visiting Angkor Wat in the 12th century would enter the temple complex by crossing a square, 600-foot-wide moat that ran some four miles in perimeter around the temple grounds. Approaching from the west, visitors would tread the moat's causeway to the main gateway. From there, they would follow a spiritual journey representing the path from the outside world through the Hindu universe and into Mount Meru, the home of the gods. They would pass a giant statue of an eight-armed Vishnu as they entered the western *gopura*, or gatehouse, known as the Entrance of the Elephants. They would then follow a stone walkway decorated with *nagas* (mythical serpents) past sunken pools and column-studded buildings once believed to house sacred temple documents.

At the end of the stone walkway, a pilgrim would step up to a rectangular platform surrounded with galleries featuring six-foot-high bas-reliefs of gods and kings. One depicts the "Churning of the Ocean of Milk," a Hindu story in which gods and demons churn a serpent in an ocean of milk to extract the elixir of life. Another illustrates the epic battle of monkey warriors against demons whose sovereign had kidnapped Sita, Rama's beautiful wife. Others depict the gruesome fates awaiting the wicked in the afterlife.

A visitor to King Suryavarman's kingdom would next ascend the dangerously steep steps to the temple's second level, an enclosed area boasting a courtyard decorated with hundreds of dancing *apsaras*, female images ornamented with jewelry and elaborately dressed hair.

For kings and high priests, the journey would continue with a climb up more steep steps to a 126-foot-high central temple, the pinnacle of Khmer society. Spreading out some 145 feet on each side, the square temple includes a courtyard cornered by four high conical towers shaped to look like lotus buds. The center of the temple is dominated by a fifth conical tower soaring 180 feet above the main causeway; inside it holds a golden statue of the Khmer patron, Vishnu, riding a half-man, half-bird creature in the image of King Suryavarman.

DISUSE AND DESTRUCTION

With the decline of the Khmer Empire and the resurgence of Buddhism, Angkor Wat was occupied by Buddhist monks, who claimed it as their own for many years. A cruciform gallery leading to the temple's second level was decorated with 1,000 Buddhas; the Vishnu statue in the central tower was replaced by an image of Buddha. The temple fell into various states of disrepair over the centuries and is now the focus of international restoration efforts.

THE MYSTERIOUS AREA 51

Who killed JFK? Did Americans really land on the moon? Conspiracy theorists have been debating these questions for years. But they all agree on one thing—these conspiracies pale in comparison to the mother of all conspiracies: Area 51.

Alien autopsies. Covert military operations. Tests on bizarre aircraft. These are all things rumored to be going on inside Area 51—a top secret location inside the Nevada Test and Training Range (NTTR) about an hour northwest of Las Vegas. Though shrouded in secrecy, some of the history of Area 51 is known. For instance, this desert area was used as a bombing test site during World War II, but no facility existed on the site until 1955. At that time, the area was chosen as the perfect location to develop and test the U-2 spy plane. Originally known as Watertown, it came to be called Area 51 in 1958 when 38,000 acres were designated for military use. The entire area was simply marked Area 51 on military maps. Today, the facility is rumored to contain approximately 575 square miles. But you won't find it on a map because, officially, it doesn't exist.

AN IMPENETRABLE FORTRESS

Getting a clear idea of the size of Area 51, or even a glimpse of the place, is next to impossible. Years ago, curiosity seekers could get a good view of the facility by hiking to the top of two nearby mountain peaks known as White Sides and Freedom Ridge. But government officials soon grew weary of people climbing up there and snapping pictures, so in 1995, they seized control of both. Currently, the only way to legally catch a glimpse of the base is to scale 7,913-foot-tall Tikaboo Peak. Even if you make it that far, you're still not guaranteed to see anything because the facility is more than 25 miles away and is only visible on clear days with no haze.

The main entrance to Area 51 is along Groom Lake Road. Those brave (or foolhardy) souls who have ventured down the road to investigate quickly realize they are being watched. Video cameras and motion sensors are hidden along the road, and signs alert the curious that if they continue any further, they will be entering a military installation, which is illegal "without the written permission of the installation commander." If that's not enough to get unwanted guests to turn around, one sign clearly states: "Use of deadly force authorized." Simply put, take one step over that imaginary line in the dirt, and they will get you.

CAMO DUDES

And just exactly who are "they"? They are the "Camo Dudes," mysterious figures watching trespassers from nearby hillsides and jeeps. If they spot something suspicious, they might call for backup—Blackhawk helicopters that will come in for a closer look. All things considered, it would probably be best to just turn around and go back home. And lest you think about hiring someone to fly you over Area 51, the entire area is considered restricted air space, meaning that unauthorized aircraft are not permitted to fly over, or even near, the facility.

WHO WORKS THERE?

Most employees are general contractors who work for companies in the area. But rather than allow these workers to commute individually, the facility has them ushered in secretly and en masse in one of two ways. The first is a mysterious white bus with tinted windows that picks up employees at several unmarked stops before whisking them through the front gates of the facility. Every evening, the bus leaves the facility and drops the employees off.

The second mode of commuter transport, an even more secretive way, is JANET, the code name given to the secret planes that carry workers back and forth from Area 51 and Las Vegas McCarran Airport. JANET has its own terminal, which is located at the far end of the airport behind fences with special security gates. It even has its own private parking lot. Several times a day, planes from the JANET fleet take off and land at the airport.

BOB LAZAR

The most famous Area 51 employee is someone who may or may not have actually worked there. In the late 1980s, Bob Lazar claimed that he'd worked at the secret facility he referred to as S-4. In addition, Lazar said that he was assigned the task of reverse engineering a recovered spaceship in order to determine how it worked. Lazar had only been at the facility for a short time, but he and his team had progressed to the point where they were test flying the alien spaceship. That's when Lazar made a big mistake. He decided to bring some friends out to Groom Lake Road when he knew the alien craft was being flown. He was caught and subsequently fired.

During his initial interviews with a local TV station, Lazar seemed credible and quite knowledgeable as to the inner workings of Area 51. But when people started trying to verify the information Lazar was giving, not only was it next to impossible to confirm most of his story, his education and employment history could not be verified either. Skeptics immediately proclaimed that Lazar was a fraud. To this day, Lazar contends that everything he said was factual and that the government deleted all his records in order to set him up and make him look like a fake. Whether or not he's telling the truth, Lazar will be remembered as the man who first brought up the idea that alien spaceships were being experimented on at Area 51.

WHAT'S REALLY GOING ON?

So what really goes on inside Area 51? One thing we do know is that they work on and test aircraft. Whether they are alien spacecraft or not is still open to debate. Some of the planes worked on and tested at Area 51 include the SR-71 Blackbird and the F-117 Nighthawk stealth fighter. Currently, there are rumors that a craft known only by the codename Aurora is being worked on at the facility.

If you want to try and catch a glimpse of some of these strange craft being tested, you'll need to hang out at the "Black Mailbox" along Highway 375, also known as the Extraterrestrial Highway. It's really nothing more than a mailbox along the side of the road. But as with most things associated with Area 51, nothing is as it sounds, so it should come as no surprise that the Black Mailbox is actually white. It belongs to a rancher, who owns the property nearby. Still, this is the spot where people have been known to camp out all night just for a chance to see something strange floating in the night sky.

THE LAWSUIT

In 1994, a landmark lawsuit was filed against the U.S. Air Force by five unnamed contractors and the widows of two others. The suit claimed that the contractors had been present at Area 51 when large quantities of "unknown chemicals" were burned in trenches and pits.

As a result of coming into contact with the fumes of the chemicals, the suit alleged that two of the contractors died, and the five survivors suffered respiratory problems and skin sores. Reporters worldwide jumped on the story, not only because it proved that Area 51 existed but also because the suit was asking for many classified documents to be entered as evidence. Would some of those documents refer to alien beings or spacecraft? The world would never know because in September 1995, while petitions for the case were still going on, President Bill Clinton signed Presidential Determination No. 95–45, which basically stated that Area 51 was exempt from federal, state, local, and interstate hazardous and solid waste laws. Shortly thereafter, the lawsuit was dismissed due to a lack of evidence, and all attempts at appeals were rejected. In 2002, President George W. Bush renewed Area 51's exemptions, ensuring once and for all that what goes on inside Area 51 stays inside Area 51.

So at the end of the day, we're still left scratching our heads about Area 51. We know it exists and we have some idea of what goes on there, but there is still so much more we don't know. More than likely, we never will know everything, but then again, what fun is a mystery if you know all the answers?

THE MYSTERIOUS BLUE HOLE

State Route 269 hides a roadside attraction of dubious depth and mysterious origin, a supposedly bottomless pool of water that locals simply call the "Blue Hole."

Every state has its tourist traps and bizarre little roadside attractions that are just intriguing enough to pull the car over to see. Back in the day, no roadside attraction brought in the Ohio travelers more than a bottomless pond filled with blue water: the mysterious and seemingly bottomless Blue Hole of Castalia.

THE BLUE HOLE'S ORIGINS

The Blue Hole is believed to have formed around 1820, when a dam burst and spilled water into a nearby hole. The ground surrounding Castalia is filled with limestone, which does not absorb groundwater well. The water quickly erodes the limestone, forming cave-ins and sinkholes. It wouldn't be until the late 1870s, however, that most people were made aware of the Blue Hole's existence; the hole was in a very isolated location in the woods. Once the Cold Creek Trout Club opened up near-by, however, its members began taking boat trips out to see the hole, and people all over the area were talking about the mysterious Blue Hole hiding out in Castalia. In 1914, a cave-in resulted in the Blue Hole growing to its current size of almost 75 feet in diameter.

STOP AND SEE THE MYSTERY

The owners of the property where the Blue Hole is situated began promoting it as a tourist stop beginning in the 1920s. It didn't hurt that the entrance to the Blue Hole property was along State Route 269, the same road that people took to get to Cedar Point amusement park. It is estimated that, at the height of its popularity, close to 165,000 people a year came out to take a peek at the Blue Hole.

The Blue Hole was promoted as being bottomless. Other strange stories were often played up as well, including the fact that the water temperature remained at 48 degrees Fahrenheit year-round. Tour guides would point out that regardless of periods of extreme rainfall or even droughtlike conditions, the Blue Hole's water level remained the same throughout.

SO WHAT'S UP WITH THIS HOLE, ANYWAY?

Despite the outlandish claims and theories surrounding the Blue Hole and its origins, the facts themselves are rather mundane. The Blue Hole is really nothing more than a freshwater pond. It isn't even bottomless. Sure, the bright blue surface of the water does indeed make the hole appear infinitely deep, but in fact, it's really only about 45 feet to the bottom at its deepest parts.

The blue color of the water is from an extremely high concentration of several elements, including lime, iron, and magnesium. That's the main reason there are no fish in the Blue Hole; they just can't survive with all that stuff in the water.

ONE HOLE OR TWO?

During the 1990s, the owners of the Blue Hole fell on hard times, forcing them to close the attraction. Families who would show up at the front entrance were forced to stare sadly through a locked gate at the small trail into the woods. That is until several years ago, when the nearby Castalia State Fish Hatchery began clearing land to expand its hatchery. Lo and behold, workers uncovered a second Blue Hole.

Just how this second Blue Hole came to be is still unknown, although the popular belief is that both holes are fed by the same underground water supply. None of that seems to matter to the Blue Hole faithful—they're just thankful to be able to take a gander at a Blue Hole again.

One of the most mystifying features of Ohio's terrain is the Hopewell Highway. Evidently the work of Native Americans between 200 BC and AD 500, it's a smooth stretch from Newark to Chillicothe. It looks very much as if it were made by human hands, suggesting a centralized, organized, sophisticated culture.

WORLD OF WONDER!

The laws of nature appear unenforceable at Mystery Hill, a popular tourist attraction in Marblehead, Ohio.

Mystery Hill is located near a limestone quarry that, for years, shipped rock throughout the Great Lakes. However, the small area of the quarry upon which Mystery Hill is located was never excavated and remained untouched. The plot was sold, and in 1953 a house was built there. Today, that's where visitors can marvel at what appears to be nature run amok. Water flows uphill, balls refuse to roll downhill, and chairs easily balance on two legs. Visitors comfortably lean at an almost 45-degree angle without falling over.

THE FOREST INSIDE THE HILL

Mystery Hill is part of a larger attraction that also includes Prehistoric Forest, a trip back in time to when dinosaurs still ruled. Sure, they're brightly painted plastic dinosaurs, but they're life-size and still pretty impressive—especially when they roar.

Visitors to Prehistoric Forest enter through a volcano and walk under a thundering waterfall where a huge serpent lies in wait. The ten-acre park is a tranquil natural forest that harkens back to Ohio's earliest days. Dinosaurs and other prehistoric creatures lurk among the trees, ready to give guests a fright, and there's also a dig site where youngsters can search for plastic dinosaur bones. Further exploration will reveal such ancient mysteries as Water Wars and miniature golf. There are other bizarre, gravity-defying locations found in Lake Wales, Florida, and Santa Cruz, California, among others. But at Mystery Hill, as it is with much of the unexplained phenomena in Ohio, the mystery and wonder of the natural world can't overcome an Ohioan's entrepreneurial spirit.

LEGENDARY LAKE MILLS

Along the interstate between Madison and Milwaukee is the small town that dubbed itself Legendary Lake Mills. It's legendary, indeed, and controversial too.

AN UNDERWATER MYSTERY

Since the 1840s, locals have buzzed about "stone tepees" standing at the bottom of Rock Lake. The idea seems plausible. Less than three miles due east is Aztalan State Park, an archeological site where the ancient remains of a Middle-Mississippian village, temple mounds, and ceremonial complex have been restored.

But Native American legend and local folklore, combined with years of third-party research, have not been enough to persuade top scientists that there are pyramids beneath Rock Lake's waters. In fact, the phenomena has been dubbed "North America's most controversial underwater archeological discovery of the 20th century."

One theory holds that Ancient Aztecs believed that their ancestors hailed from a land far north of Mexico, called Aztalan. The legend goes that in 1066, the Aztalans of Lake Mills appealed to the gods for relief from a long drought by building sacrificial pyramids. Rain came down, creating a beautiful lake and submerging the pyramids. They named the lake Tyranena, meaning "sparkling waters."

Fast-forward 800 years. When the first white settlers set up camp along Tyranena's banks in the 1830s, the resident Winnebago people shared the story of Tyranena with them. But even the Winnebago didn't quite understand the story, as it came from a "foreign tribe." The lore remained as elusive as the small islands that settlers reported as floating above the water.

Soon after the settlers arrived, a sawmill and a gristmill were built on the lake's edge, subsequently raising the water level. What little was left to see of the supposed pyramids was submerged.

DOUBT AND CIRCUMSTANCE

Over the next 200 years, the lake would be caught up in a continuous cycle of sensationalism and doubt, false starts, and circumstance. In the early 1900s, two brothers, Claude and Lee Wilson, went out duck hunting one hot, clear day during adrought and were able to reach down and touch the so-called pyramid's apex with an oar. Local residents would find the pyramid again the next day, but by the time a reporter got onto the lake a week later rain had fallen, ending the drought and raising the water level. Through the decades, anglers would declare their belief in the structures when they snagged their lines and nets, but interest waned.

The lore was rekindled in the 1930s when a local schoolteacher, Victor Taylor, took it upon himself to canvass residents and dive over the pyramids, without diving equipment. He described four conical underwater structures. With this "evidence," state and national agencies threw money into the effort, even hiring professional divers to explore the underwater structures. But these divers were literally mired by the lake's deteriorating, muddy bottom, mucking up belief in the pyramids once again.

Eventually the controversy would reach an MIT engineer, Max Nohl, the man who invented the first scuba-type device. A master excavator, Nohl made it his personal mission to uncover the truth beneath the lake. He rekindled the town's pyramid fever with his extensive dives and written accounts with detailed measurements.

DEBUNKED?

While Nohl successfully made his case, the curious fact remained that no professional archeologist wanted to be associated with Rock Lake. The establishment theory contends that the lake bottom anomalies are merely glacial castoffs from the last Ice Age. In an article in the September 1962 issue of *The Wisconsin Archeologist*, the pyramids were wholly debunked by the state's academes, who alleged that Native Americans didn't work in stone and that mound-building only began 2,000 years prior, whereas Rock Lake was at least 10,000 years old. Case closed. Or not.

In July 1967, Jack Kennedy, a professional diver from Illinois, was sport diving with friends on Rock Lake. Near the end of the day, after all of his comrades had run out of air, Kennedy took one last dive...over a pyramid. Shocked at his discovery, he removed three rocks from its wall. Further analysis revealed the rocks were made of quartzite from a riverbed. The first concrete evidence was now in hand.

Kennedy continued to dive at Rock Lake, eventually making a sketch of a structure 70 feet long, 30 feet wide, and 15 feet tall, which appeared in *Skin Diver* magazine. His discovery led to a resurgence in the exploration of Rock Lake, a summer haven for leisure boaters and beachgoers. Explorers have documented stone rings, tombs, curiously long rock bars, and pyramidal structures in dives, sonic sonar, and aerial photography. In 1998, two Rock Lake enthusiasts, Archie Eschborn and Jack LeTourneau, formed Rock Lake Research Society to "document and help preserve these archeological treasures that could rewrite North American history...and persuade state officials to declare Rock Lake a historical site."

HISTORY STILL UNWRITTEN

Does the Aztalan connection hold water? How does glacial activity fit in the picture?

To date, Rock Lake remains just that, a lake, which is still unprotected as a historical site. But locals continue to believe, if not for the archeological and anthropological truth, then for the opportunities the lore and legend provide. In Lake Mills, you can stay at the Pyramid Motel or throw back a Stone Tepee Pale Ale, made by the city's resident Tyranena Brewing Company. Or perhaps you can head to one of the city's three beaches and try your hand at uncovering the mysteries of the "sparkling waters" yourself.

THE LIBRARY OF THE MUSES

By far the most famous library in history, the Library of Alexandria held an untold number of ancient works. Its fiery destruction meant the irrecoverable loss of a substantial part of the world's intellectual history.

THE LIBRARY'S BEGINNINGS

The cities of ancient Mesopotamia (e.g., Uruk, Nineveh, Babylon) and Egypt (e.g., Thebes, Memphis) had cultivated archives and libraries since the Bronze Age, but the idea for a library as grand as Alexandria did not occur in Greek culture until the Hellenistic Age, when Alexander the Great's conquests brought both Greece and these former civilizations under Macedonian rule. Previous Greek libraries were owned by individuals; the largest belonged to Aristotle (384–322 BC), whose work and school (the Lyceum) in Athens were supported by Alexander.

When Alexander died suddenly in 323 BC, his generals

carved his empire into regional dynasties. The Hellenistic dynasties competed with each other for three centuries (until each was in turn conquered by either Rome or Parthia). Each dynasty desired cultural dominance, so they invited famous artists, authors, and intellectuals to live and work in their capital cities. Alexander's general Ptolemy, who controlled Egypt, decided to develop a collection of the world's learning (the Library) and a research center, the Mouseion (the Museum, or Temple of the Muses), where scholars on subsidy could study and add their research to the collection. This idea may well have come from Demetrius of Phaleron (350–280 BC), Ptolemy's advisor and the former governor of Athens, who had been a pupil at the Lyceum, but the grand project became one of the hallmarks of the Ptolemaic dynasty. Under the first three Ptolemies, the Museum, a royal library, and a smaller "daughter" library at the Temple of Serapis (the Serapeum) were built and grew as Alexandria became the intellectual, as well as commercial, capital of the Hellenistic world.

Egypt and Alexandria offered the Ptolemies distinct advantages for accomplishing their goals. Egypt was not only immensely rich, which gave it the wealth to purchase materials and to bring scholars to Alexandria, but it was the major producer of papyrus, a marsh reed that was beaten into a flat surface and made into scrolls for writing and copying. Alexandria was also the commercial hub of the Mediterranean, and goods and information from all over the world passed through its port.

BIBLIOMANIA: SO MANY SCROLLS, SO LITTLE TIME

Acquiring materials for the libraries and Museum became somewhat of an obsession for the Ptolemies. Although primarily focused on Greek and Egyptian works, their interests included translating other traditions into Greek. Among the most important of these efforts was the production of the Septuagint, a Greek version of the Jewish scriptures. Besides employing agents to scour major book markets and to search out copies of works not yet in the library, boats coming into Alexandria were required to declare any scrolls on board. If they were of interest, the scrolls were confiscated and copied, and the owners were given the copies and some compensation. Ptolemy III (285–222 BC) may have acquired Athens' official state collection of the plays of Aeschylus, Sophocles, and Euripides in a similar way—putting up 15 talents of silver as a guarantee while he had the plays copied, then foregoing the treasure in favor of keeping the originals. Whether or not this is true, it speaks to the value he placed on getting important works and the resources he had at his disposal to do so.

Alexandria's efforts were fueled by a fierce competition with the Hellenistic kingdom of Pergamum (modern Bergamo, Turkey), which created its own library. Each library sought to claim new finds and to produce new editions, leading at times to the acquisition of forgeries and occasional embarrassment. Alexandria finally tried to undercut its rival by cutting off papyrus exports, but Pergamum perfected a method for making writing material out of animal skins (now called "parchment" from the Latin *pergamina*) and continued to build its holdings. Eventually, however, Alexandria got the upper hand when the Roman general Marcus Antonius (Mark Antony) conquered Pergamum and made a present of its library to his lover, the Ptolemaic Queen Cleopatra.

Estimates as to the number of volumes in the Alexandrian library ranged wildly even in antiquity, generally between 200,000 and 700,000. Estimates are complicated by the fact that it isn't clear whether the numbers originate from works or scrolls: Some scrolls contained one work, some multiple works, and long works like the Iliad took multiple scrolls. Over time, a complex cataloguing system evolved, which culminated in a bibliographic survey of the library's holdings called the Pinakes. The survey was put together by the great Hellenistic scholar and poet Callimachus of Cyrene (305–240 BC). Unfortunately, this important work only exists in fragments today.

BURNING DOWN THE HOUSE

The Royal Library and its holdings were accidentally set aflame in 48 BC when Caesar tried to burn his way out of being trapped in the port by opposing forces. Further losses probably occurred in AD 271 when Emperor Aurelian destroyed part of the Museum while recapturing Alexandria from Queen Zenobia's forces. The "daughter" library of the Serapeum was finally destroyed by Christians under Emperor Theodosius near the end of the 4th century. But by then, much of the contents had decayed or found their way into other hands, leaving the classical heritage scattered and fragmented for centuries. Much later, Christians dramatically blamed the burning of the library holdings on Muslim conquerors.

CHAPTER 5

URBAN LEGENDS, CURSES, & CLANDESTINE TRADITIONS

SATANIC MARKETING

What's behind the vicious rumor that put mega-corporation Procter & Gamble on many churches' hit lists?

Procter & Gamble, one of the largest corporations in the world, manufactures a plethora of products that range from pet food to potato chips. The company takes pride in its reputation as a business that can be trusted, so it came as a huge shock when, starting in the 1960s, Christian churches and individuals around the country spread the rumor that P&G was dedicated to the service of Satan.

THE DEVIL IS IN THE DETAILS

How the rumor got started remains a mystery. According to one of the most popular versions of the story, the president of P&G appeared on *The Phil Donahue Show* in March 1994 and announced that, because of society's new openness, he finally felt comfortable revealing that he was a member of the Church of Satan and that much of his company's profits went toward the advancement of that organization. When Donahue supposedly asked him whether such an announcement would have a negative impact on P&G, the CEO replied, "There aren't enough Christians in the United States to make a difference."

There's one problem with this story—and with the variations that place the company president on *The Sally Jessy Raphael Show*, *The Merv Griffin Show*, and *60 Minutes*: It didn't happen.

LOSE THE LOGO

Adding fuel to the fable was the company's logo, which featured the image of a "man in the moon" and 13 stars. Many interpreted this rather innocuous design to be Satanic, and some even claimed that the curlicues in the man's beard looked like the number 666—the biblical "mark of the Beast" referred to in the Book of Revelation. By 1985, the company had become so frustrated by the allegations that it had no choice but to retire the logo, which had graced P&G products for more than 100 years.

SPEAKING OUT

Procter & Gamble did all it could to quell the rumors, which resulted in more than 200,000 phone calls and letters from concerned consumers. Company spokespeople vehemently denied the story, explaining in a press release: "The president of P&G has never discussed Satanism on any national televised talk show, nor has any other P&G executive. The moon-and-stars trademark dates back to the mid-1800s, when the 'man in the moon' was simply a popular design. The 13 stars in the design honor the original 13 colonies."

In addition, the company turned to several prominent religious leaders, including evangelist Billy Graham, to help clear its name, and when that didn't work, it even sued a handful of clergy members who continued to spread the offending story.

Talk show host Sally Jessy Raphael also denied the allegations, noting, "The rumors going around that the president of Procter & Gamble appeared on [my] show and announced he was a member of the Church of Satan are not true. The president of Procter & Gamble has never appeared on *The Sally Jessy Raphael Show*."

SENSELESS ALLEGATIONS

Of course, like most urban legends, this story falls apart under the slightest scrutiny. Foremost, one must ask why the CEO of an international conglomerate (especially one that must answer to stockholders) would risk decades of consumer goodwill—not to mention billions of dollars in sales—to announce to the world that his company was run by and catered to Satanists. And even if that were the case, he needn't bother announcing it, since any deals made with the devil would be a matter of public record.

❖ In 2007, a jury awarded Procter & Gamble $19.25 million in a civil lawsuit filed against four former Amway distributors accused of spreading false rumors about the company's ties to the Church of Satan. The distributors were found guilty of using a voicemail system to inform customers that P&G's profits were used to support Satanic cults.

THE MYSTERY OF THE 700-YEAR-OLD PIPER

It's an intriguing story about a mysterious piper and more than 100 missing children. Made famous by the eponymous Brothers Grimm, this popular fairy tale has captivated generations of boys and girls. But is it actually more fact than fiction?

The legend of The Pied Piper of Hameln documents the story of a mysterious musician who rid a town of rats by enchanting the rodents with music from his flute. The musician led the mesmerized rats to a nearby river, where they drowned. When the townsfolk refused to settle their debt, the rat catcher returned several weeks later, charmed a group of 130 children with the same flute, and led them out of town. They disappeared—never to be seen again.

It's a story that dates back to approximately AD 1300 and has its roots in a small German town called Hameln. Several accounts written between the 14th and 17th centuries tell of a stained-glass window in the town's main church. The window pictured the Pied Piper with hands clasped, standing over a group of youngsters. Encircling the window was the following verse (this is a rough translation): "In the year 1284, on John's and Paul's day was the 26th of June. By a piper, dressed in all kinds of colors, 130 children born in Hameln were seduced and lost at the calvarie near the koppen."

The verse is quite specific: precise month and year, exact number of children involved in the incident, and detailed place names. Because of this, some scholars believe this window, which was removed in 1660 and either accidentally destroyed or lost, was created in memory of an actual event. Yet, the verse makes no mention of the circumstances regarding the departure of the children or their specific fate. What exactly happened in Hameln, Germany, in 1284? The truth is, no one actually knows—at least not for certain.

THEORIES ABOUND

Gernot Hüsam, the current chairman of the Coppenbrügge Castle Museum, believes the word *koppen* in the inscription may reference a rocky outcrop on a hill in nearby Coppenbrügge, a small town previously known as Koppanberg. Hüsam also believes the use of the word *calvarie* is in reference to either the medieval connotation of the gates of hell—or since the Crusades—a place of execution.

One theory put forward is that Coppenbrügge resident Nikolaus von Spiegelberg recruited Hameln youth to emigrate to areas in Pomerania near the Baltic Sea. This theory suggests the youngsters were either murdered, because they took part in summertime pagan rituals, or drowned in a tragic accident while in transit to the new colonies.

But this is not the only theory. In fact, theories concerning the fate of the children abound. Here are some ideas about what really happened:

❖ They suffered from the Black Plague or a similar disease and were led from the town to spare the rest of the population.

❖ They were part of a crusade to the Holy Land.

❖ They were lost in the 1260 Battle of Sedemünder.

❖ They died in a bridge collapse over the Weser River or a landslide on Ith Mountain.

❖ They emigrated to settle in other parts of Europe, including Maehren, Oelmutz, Transylvania, or Uckermark.

❖ They were actually young adults who were led away and murdered for performing pagan rituals on a local mountain.

Historians believe that emigration, bridge collapse/natural disaster, disease, or murder are the most plausible explanations.

TRACING THE PIPER'S PATH

Regardless of what actually happened in Hameln hundreds of years ago, the legend of the Pied Piper has endured. First accounts of the Piper had roots to the actual incident, but as time passed, the story took on a life of its own.

Earliest accounts of the legend date back to 1384, at which time a Hameln church leader, Deacon von Lude, was said to be in possession of a chorus book with a Latin verse related to the legend written on the front cover by his grandmother. The book was misplaced in the late 17th century and has never been found.

The oldest surviving account—according to amateur Pied Piper historian Jonas Kuhn—appears as an addition to a 14th-century manuscript from Luneburg. Written in Latin, the note is almost identical to the verse on the stained-glass window and translates roughly to:

"In the year of 1284, on the day of Saints John and Paul on the 26th of June 130 children born in Hamelin were seduced By a piper, dressed in all kinds of colors, and lost at the place of execution near the koppen."

The 16th-century physician and philosopher Jobus Fincelius believed the Pied Piper was the devil. In his 1556 book, *Concerning the Wonders of His Times*, Fincelius wrote: "It came about in Hameln in Saxony on the River Weser...the Devil visibly in human form walked the lanes of Hameln and by playing a pipe lured after him many children...to a mountain. Once there, he with the children...could no longer be found."

In 1557, Count Froben Christoph von Zimmern wrote a chronicle detailing his family's lineage. Sprinkled throughout the book were several folklore tales including one that referenced the Pied Piper. For some unknown reason, the count introduced rats into his version of the story: "He passed through the streets of the town with his small pipe...immediately all the rats...collected outside the houses and followed his footsteps." This first insertion of rodents into the legend led other writers to follow suit.

In 1802, Johan Wolfgang Goethe wrote "Der Rattenfanger," a poem based on the legend. The monologue was told in the first person through the eyes of the rat catcher. Goethe's poem made no direct reference to the town of Hameln, and in Goethe's version the Piper played a stringed instrument instead of a pipe. The Piper also made an appearance in Goethe's literary work *Faust*.

Jacob and Wilhelm Grimm began collecting European folktales in the early 1800s. Best known for a series of books that documented 211 fairy tales, the brothers also published two volumes between 1816 and 1818 detailing almost 600 German folklore legends. One of the volumes contained the story of "Der Rattenfanger von Hameln."

The Grimm brothers' research for *The Pied Piper* drew on 11 different sources, from which they deduced two children were left behind (a blind child and a mute child); the piper led the children through a cave to Transylvania; and a street in Hameln was named after the event.

NO END IN SIGHT

While the details of the historical event surrounding the legend of The Pied Piper have been lost to time, the mystique of the story endures. Different versions of the legend have even appeared in literature outside of Germany: A rat catcher from Vienna helped rid the nearby town of Korneuburg of rats. When he wasn't paid, he stole off with the town's children and sold them as slaves in Constantinople. A vagabond rid the English town of

Newton on the Isle of Wight of their rats, and when he wasn't paid, led the town's children into an ancient oak forest where they were never seen again. A Chinese version had a Hangchow district official use magic to convince the rats to leave his city.

The legend's plot has been adapted over time to fit whichever media is currently popular and has been used as a story line in children's books, ballet, theatre, and even a radio drama. The intriguing story of the mysterious piper will continue to interest people as long as there is mystery surrounding the original event.

THE CURSE OF KING TUT'S TOMB

If you discovered a mummy's tomb, would you go in? The curse of King Tut's tomb is a classic tale, even if there's a lot of evidence that says there was never anything to worry about. Still…would you wanna go in there?

CURSE, SCHMURSE!

In the early 1920s, English explorer and archeologist Howard Carter led an expedition funded by the Fifth Earl of Carnarvon to unearth the tomb of Egyptian King Tutankhamun. Most of the tombs of Egyptian kings had been ransacked long ago, but Carter had reason to believe that King Tut's 3,000-year-old tomb was probably still full of artifacts from the ancient world. He was right.

Within the king's burial chamber were vases, precious metals, statues, even whole chariots—all buried with the king to aid him in the afterlife. Carter and his team excavated to their heart's content, and due to their hard work, we now know a great deal more about the life of ancient Egyptian people during King Tut's time.

Carter had been warned about the dangers of disrupting an ancient tomb, but he didn't buy into the rumors of curses and hexes. After opening the tomb, however, it was hard to deny that some strange, unpleasant events began to take place in the lives of those involved in the expedition.

CURSE OR COINCIDENCE?

During the 1920s, several men involved in the excavation died shortly after entering King Tut's tomb. The first one to go—the Fifth Earl of Carnarvon—died only a few months after completing the excavation. Legend has it that at the exact moment the earl died, all the lights in the city of Cairo mysteriously went out. That morning, his dog allegedly dropped dead, too.

Egyptologists claim that the spores and mold released from opening an ancient grave are often enough to make a person sick or worse. The earl had been suffering from a chronic illness before he left for Egypt, which could have made him more susceptible to the mold, and, therefore, led to his death.

Other stories say that the earl was bitten by a mosquito. Considering the sanitary conditions in Egypt at the time, a mosquito bite in Cairo could have some serious consequences, including malaria and other deadly diseases. Some reports indicate that the bite became infected and he died as a result—not because an ancient pharaoh was annoyed with him.

There were other odd happenings, and the public, already interested in the discovery of the tomb itself, was hungry for details of "the curse of the pharaohs." Newspapers reported all kinds of "proof": the earl's younger brother died suddenly five months after the excavation, and on the morning of the opening of the tomb, Carter's pet bird was swallowed by a cobra—the same kind of vicious cobra depicted on the mask of King Tut. Two of the workers hired for the dig died after opening the tomb, though their passing was likely due to malaria, not any curse.

Six of the 26 explorers involved died within a decade. But many of those involved in the exploration lived long, happy lives, including Carter. He never paid much attention to the curse, and, apparently, it never paid much attention to him. In 1939, Carter died of natural causes at age 64, after working with King Tut and his treasures for more than 17 years.

YEAH, RIGHT

King Tutankhamun's sarcophagus and treasures have toured the world on a nearly continual basis since their discovery and restoration. When the exhibit went to America in the 1970s, some people tried to revive the old curse. When a San Francisco police officer suffered a mild stroke while guarding a gold funeral mask, he unsuccessfully tried to collect compensation, claiming his stroke was due to the pharaoh's curse.

ARF! DOG-MEN IN HISTORY

Dog may be man's best friend, but he's also been invoked to explain the unexplainable, and even to denigrate enemies—reasons why tales of men with the heads of dogs are not uncommon throughout the historical record.

DOG-HEADED FOREIGNERS

Ancient stories about dog-headed men unwittingly reveal an apprehensiveness about the power of canines. We love our pooches, but let's face it: They have claws and sharp teeth, they run faster than we do, and they can eat our faces if they feel like it. Historically, this small bit of disquiet bubbling beneath our adoration has encouraged cultures to invoke doglike creatures for diverse purposes, sometimes as gods, such as Egypt's Anubis, and frequently to belittle other cultures.

Whatever the motives, the eventual effect of these pervasive tales was to make fantastical dog-men seem very real. Most imaginative of all, though, were ancient writers from China, India, and Europe, who relayed purportedly true stories of human beings who literally had the heads of dogs.

SIT, CYNOCEPHALI!

Dog-headed peoples are often referred to as Cynocephali, Greek for "dog-head." In the 5th century BC, Greek historian Herodotus, "The Father of History," described a distant country inhabited by "huge snakes and the lions, and the elephants and bears and asps, the Kunokephaloi (Dog-headed) and the Headless Men that have their eyes in their chests." Herodotus was not alone in his testimony about dog-headed peoples. Fellow Greek historian Ctesias claimed that on the mountains in distant India, "there live men with the head of a dog, whose clothing is the skin of wild beasts."

In accounts of this nature, it's difficult to sort out myth from fact. Like many of today's bloggers, ancient historians made implausible claims based on hearsay rather than direct observation. Writers played so fast and loose with the available facts that many believed—and made their readers believe—that some foreign societies barked rather than spoke.

Some historians tried to legitimize their claims by skipping down the road of pseudo-science. The 2nd-century Greek historian Aelian included the Cynocephali in his book of animals. He declared that beyond Egypt one encounters the "human Kynoprosopoi (Dog faces)…they are black in appearance, and they have the head and teeth of a dog. And since they resemble this animal, it is very natural that I should mention them here [in a book about animals]."

RACISM COLLIDES WITH LEGEND

Many present-day historians charge that these accounts of dog-headed tribes aren't simply reflections of a fear of foreigners, but racist ignorance. Repeated accounts of dog-headed groups in northern Africa suggest that race did indeed help encourage some dog-driven tales. These African groups were often referred to as the Marmaritae, who engaged in on-again off-again warfare with the Romans. Legend has it that St. Christopher was a captured dog-headed slave from a Marmaritae tribe—paintings that depict the saint with the head of a brown dog still exist. According to lore, Christopher's dog head was replaced with a normal human head after he was baptized.

Modern scholars believe that historical references to dog-headed tribes derived from the lore created by many tribes in Central Asia, who described their own origins as having roots in the progeny of a human female who mated with a male dog. Biology this startling certainly would have tickled the imaginations of outsiders, and reinforced the notion that dog-headedness signified a profound and culturally expedient "otherness" of foreigners.

BAFFLING BABOONS

And then there's the issue of *Papio cynocephalus*, central Africa's yellow baboon, whose head is curiously dog-like. Foreigners' accounts of Africa often remarked on this intriguing animal with zeal. In fact, during the mad European scramble to colonize the African continent in the 19th century, baboons were shipped to the West for exhibition in circuses and freak shows as exotic dog-men. One such circus claimed that its baboon-man had been captured from an ancient African tribe. Marveling audiences failed to see the baboon face on the baboon, just as people failed to see the legitimate uniqueness of persons who didn't look or act as they did.

ONE REPTILE TO RULE THEM ALL

Some people are ruled by their pets; others are ruled by their work. Conspiracy theorist David Icke believes that we're all being ruled by reptilian humanoids.

WORLDWIDE DOMINATION

David Icke has worn many hats: journalist, news anchor for the BBC, spokesman for the British Green Party, and professional soccer player. But after a spiritual experience in Peru in 1991, he took on another role: famed conspiracy theorist.

Like many other conspiracy theorists, Icke believes that a group called the Illuminati, or "global elite," controls the world. According to these theorists, the group manipulates the economy and uses mind control to usher humanity into a submissive state. Icke also believes that the group is responsible for organizing such tragedies as the Holocaust and the Oklahoma City bombings.

Some of the most powerful people in the world are members, claims Icke, including ex-British Prime Minister Tony Blair and former U.S. President George H. W. Bush, as well as leaders of financial institutions and major media outlets. However, not all members are human. According to Icke, those at the top of the Illuminati bloodlines are vehicles for a reptilian entity from the constellation Draco. These shape-shifters can change from human to reptile and back again, and they are essentially controlling humanity.

IS ICKE ONTO SOMETHING?

In the documentary *David Icke: Was He Right?*, Icke claims that many of his earlier predictions, including a hurricane in New Orleans and a "major attack on a large city" between the years 2000 and 2002, have come true. But are we really being ruled by reptilian humanoids or is Icke's theory a bunch of snake oil? Icke was nearly laughed off the stage in a 1991 appearance on a BBC talk show. But with 16 published books, thousands attending his speaking engagements, and nearly 200,000 weekly hits to his website, perhaps it's Icke who's having the last laugh.

A FIERY DEBATE: SPONTANEOUS HUMAN COMBUSTION

Proponents contend that the phenomenon—in which a person suddenly bursts into flames—is very real. Skeptics, however, are quick to explain it away.

THE CURIOUS CASE OF HELEN CONWAY

A photo documents the gruesome death of Helen Conway. Visible in the black-and-white image—taken in 1964 in Delaware County, Pennsylvania—is an oily smear that was her torso and, behind, an ashen specter of the upholstered bedroom chair she occupied. The picture's most haunting feature might be her legs, thin and ghostly pale, clearly intact and seemingly unscathed by whatever it was that consumed the rest of her.

What consumed her, say proponents of a theory that people can catch fire without an external source of ignition, was spontaneous human combustion. It's a classic case, believers assert: Conway was immolated by an intense, precisely localized source of heat that damaged little else in the room. Adding to the mystery, the investigating fire marshal said that it took just twenty-one minutes for her to burn away and that he could not identify an outside accelerant.

If Conway's body ignited from within and burned so quickly she had no time to rise and seek help, hers wouldn't be the first or last death to fit the pattern of spontaneous human combustion.

The phenomenon was documented as early as 1763 by Frenchman Jonas Dupont in his collection of accounts, published as *De Incendis Corporis Humani Spontaneis*. Charles Dickens's 1852 novel *Bleak House* sensationalized the issue with the spontaneous-combustion death of a character named Krook. That humans have been reduced to ashes with little damage to their surroundings is not the stuff of fiction, however. Many documented cases exist. The question is, did these people combust spontaneously?

HOW IT HAPPENS

Theories advancing the concept abound. Early hypotheses held that victims, such as Dickens's Krook, were likely alcoholics so besotted that their very flesh became flammable. Later conjecture blamed the influence of geomagnetism. A 1996 book by John Heymer, *The Entrancing Flame*, maintained emotional distress could lead to explosions of defective mitochondria. These outbursts cause cellular releases of hydrogen and oxygen and trigger crematory reactions in the body. That same year, Larry E. Arnold—publicity material calls him a parascientist—published *Ablaze! The Mysterious Fires of Spontaneous Human Combustion*. Arnold claimed sufferers were struck by a subatomic particle he had discovered and named the "pyrotron."

Perhaps somewhat more credible reasoning came out of Brooklyn, New York, where the eponymous founder of Robin Beach Engineers Associated (described as a scientific detective agency) linked the theory of spontaneous human combustion with proven instances of individuals whose biology caused them to retain intense concentrations of static electricity.

A CONTROVERSY IS SPARKED

Skeptics are legion. They suspect that accounts are often embellished or important facts are ignored. That the unfortunate Helen Conway was overweight and a heavy smoker, for instance, likely played a key role in her demise.

Indeed, Conway's case is considered by some to be evidence of the wick effect, which might be today's most forensically respected explanation for spontaneous human combustion. It holds that an external source, such as a dropped cigarette, ignites bedding, clothing, or furnishings. This material acts like an absorbing wick, while the body's fat takes on the fueling role of candle wax. The burning fat liquefies, saturating the bedding, clothing, or furnishings, and keeps the heat localized.

The result is a long, slow immolation that burns away fatty tissues, organs, and associated bone, leaving leaner areas, such as legs, untouched. Experiments on pig carcasses show it can take five or more hours, with the body's water boiling off ahead of the spreading fire.

Under the wick theory, victims are likely to already be unconscious when the fire starts. They're in closed spaces with little moving air, so the flames are allowed to smolder, doing their work without disrupting the surroundings or alerting passersby.

Nevertheless, even the wick effect theory, like all other explanations of spontaneous human combustion, has scientific weaknesses. The fact remains, according to the mainstream science community, that evidence of spontaneous human combustion is entirely circumstantial, and that not a single proven eyewitness account exists to substantiate anyone's claims of "Poof—the body just went up in flames!"

"MKULTRA" SHOCK

From the mid-1950s through at least the early 1970s, thousands of unwitting Americans and Canadians became part of a bizarre CIA research project codenamed MKULTRA. Participants were secretly "brainwashed"—drugged with LSD and other hallucinogens, subjected to electro-convulsive shock therapy, and manipulated with abusive mind-control techniques.

MKULTRA began in 1953 under the orders of CIA director Allen Dulles. The program, which was in direct violation of the human rights provisions of the Nuremberg Code that the United States helped establish after WWII, was developed in response to reports that U.S. prisoners of war in Korea were being subjected to mind-control techniques.

CIA researchers hoped to find a "truth drug" that could be used on Soviet agents, as well as drugs that could be used against foreign leaders (one documented scheme involved an attempt in 1960 to dose Fidel Castro with LSD). They also aimed to develop means of mind control that would benefit U.S. intelligence. As part of MKULTRA, the CIA investigated parapsychology and such phenomena as hypnosis, telepathy, precognition, photokinesis, and remote viewing.

MKULTRA was headed by Dr. Sidney Gottlieb, a military psychiatrist and chemist known as the "Black Sorcerer," who specialized in concocting deadly poisons. More than 30 universities and scientific institutes took part in MKULTRA. LSD and other mind-altering drugs including heroin, mescaline, psilocybin, scopolamine, marijuana, and sodium pentothal were given to CIA employees, military personnel, and other government workers, often without the subjects' knowledge or prior consent. To broaden their subject pool, researchers targeted unsuspecting civilians, often those in vulnerable or socially compromising situations. Prison inmates, prostitutes, and mentally ill hospital patients were often used. In a project codenamed Operation Midnight Climax, the CIA set up brothels in several U.S. cities to lure men as unwitting test subjects. Rooms were equipped with cameras that filmed the experiments behind one-way mirrors. Some civilian subjects who consented to participation were used for more extreme experimentation. One group of volunteers in Kentucky was given LSD for more than 70 straight days.

In the 1960s, Dr. Gottlieb also traveled to Vietnam and conducted mind-control experiments on Viet Cong prisoners of war being held by U.S. forces. During the same time period, an unknown number of Soviet agents died in U.S. custody in Europe after being given dual intravenous injections of barbiturates and amphetamine in the CIA's search for a truth serum.

MKULTRA experiments were also carried out in Montreal, Canada, between 1957 and 1964 by Dr. Donald Ewen Cameron, a researcher in Albany, New York, who also served as president of the World Psychiatric Association and the American and Canadian psychiatric associations. The CIA appears to have given him potentially deadly experiments to carry out at Canadian mental health institutes so U.S. citizens would not be involved. Cameron also experimented with paralytic drugs—in some cases inducing a coma in subjects for up to three months—as well as using electro-convulsive therapy at 30 times the normal voltage. The subjects were often women being treated for anxiety disorders and postpartum depression. Many suffered permanent damage. A lawsuit by victims of the experiments later uncovered that the Canadian government had also funded the project.

At least one American subject died in the experiments. Frank Olson, a U.S. army biological weapons researcher, was secretly given LSD in 1953. A week later, he fell from a hotel window in New York City following a severe psychotic episode. A CIA doctor assigned to monitor Olson claimed he jumped from the window, but an autopsy performed on Olson's exhumed remains in 1994 found that he had been knocked unconscious before the fall.

The U.S. army also conducted experiments with psychoactive drugs. A later investigation determined that nearly all army experiments involved soldiers and civilians who had given their informed consent, and that army researchers had largely followed scientific and safety protocols. Ken Kesey, who would later write *One Flew Over the Cuckoo's Nest* and become one of the originators of the hippie movement, volunteered for LSD studies at an army research center in San Francisco in 1960. LSD stolen from the army lab by test subjects was some of the first in the world used "recreationally" by civilians. The army's high ethical standards, however, seem to have been absent in at least one case. Harold Blauer, a professional tennis player in New York City who was hospitalized for depression following his divorce, died from apparent cardiac arrest during an army experiment in 1952. Blauer had been secretly injected with massive doses of mescaline.

CIA researchers eventually concluded that the effects of LSD were too unpredictable to be useful, and the agency later acknowledged that their experiments made little scientific sense. Records on 150 MKULTRA research projects were destroyed in 1973 by order of CIA Director Richard Helms. A year later, the *New York Times* first reported about CIA experiments on U.S. citizens. In 1975, congressional hearings and a report by the Rockefeller Commission revealed details of the program. In 1976, President Gerald Ford issued an executive order prohibiting experimentation with drugs on human subjects without their informed consent. Ford and CIA Director William Colby also publicly apologized to Frank Olson's family, who received $750,000 by a special act of Congress.

Though no evidence exists that the CIA succeeded in its quest to find mind-control techniques, some conspiracy theories claim that the MKULTRA project was linked to the assassination of Robert F. Kennedy. Some have argued that Kennedy's assassin, Sirhan B. Sirhan, had been subjected to mind control. Sirhan claims that he has no recollection of shooting Kennedy, despite attempts by both government prosecutors and his defense lawyers to use hypnosis to recover his memories.

TO THE MOON!

Television and film star Jackie Gleason was fascinated with the paranormal and UFOs. But he had no idea that an innocent game with an influential friend would lead him face-to-face with his obsession.

Jackie Gleason was a star of the highest order. The rotund actor kept television audiences in stitches with his portrayal of hardheaded but ultimately lovable family man Ralph Kramden in the 1955 sitcom *The Honeymooners*. He made history with his regularly aimed, but never delivered, threats to TV wife Alice, played by Audrey Meadows: "One of these days Alice, one of these days, pow, right in the kisser," and "Bang, zoom! To the moon, Alice!"

But many fans didn't know that Gleason was obsessed with the supernatural, and he owned a massive collection of memorabilia on the subject. It was so large and impressive that the University of Miami, Florida, put it on permanent exhibit after his death in 1987. He even had a house built in the shape of a UFO, which he christened "The Mothership." The obsession was legendary, and it climaxed in an unimaginable way.

A HIGH STAKES GAME

An avid golfer, Gleason also kept a home close to Inverrary Golf and Country Club in Lauderhill, Florida. A famous golfing buddy lived nearby—U.S. President Richard M. Nixon, who had a compound on nearby Biscayne Bay. The Hollywood star and the controversial politician shared a love of the links, politics, and much more.

The odyssey began when Gleason and Nixon met for a golf tournament at Inverrary in February 1973. Late in the day their conversation turned to a topic close to Gleason's heart—UFOs. To the funnyman's surprise, the president revealed his own fascination with the subject, touting a large collection of books that rivaled Gleason's. They talked shop through the rest of the game, but Gleason noticed reservation in Nixon's tone, as if the aides and security within earshot kept the president from speaking his mind. He would soon learn why.

Later that evening around midnight, an unexpected guest visited the Gleason home. It was Nixon, alone. The customary secret service detail assigned to him was nowhere to be seen. Confused, Gleason asked Nixon the reason for such a late call. He replied only that he had to show Gleason something. They climbed into Nixon's private car and sped off. The drive brought them to Homestead Air Force Base in South Miami-Dade County. Nixon took them to a large, heavily guarded building. Guards parted as the pair headed inside the structure, Gleason following Nixon past labs before arriving at a series of large cases. The cases held wreckage from a downed UFO, Nixon told his friend. Seeing all of this, Gleason had his doubts and imagined himself the target of an elaborated staged hoax.

Leaving the wreckage, the pair entered a chamber holding six (some reports say eight) freezers topped with thick glass. Peering into the hulls, Gleason later said he saw dead bodies—but not of the human variety. The remains were small, almost childlike in stature, but withered in appearance and possessing only three or four digits per hand. They were also severely mangled, as if they had been in a devastating accident.

Returning home, Gleason was giddy. His obsession had come full circle. The enthusiasm changed in the weeks that followed, however, shifting to intense fear and worry. A patriotic American, Gleason couldn't reconcile his government's secrecy about the UFO wreckage. Traumatized, he began drinking heavily and suffered from severe insomnia.

THE "TRUTH" COMES OUT

Gleason kept details of his wild night with Nixon under wraps. Unfortunately, his soon-to-be-ex-wife didn't follow his lead. Beverly Gleason spilled the beans in *Esquire* magazine and again in an unpublished memoir on her marriage to Gleason. Supermarket tabloids ate the story up. Gleason only opened up about his night with Nixon in the last weeks of his life. Speaking to Larry Warren, a former Air Force pilot with his own UFO close encounter, a slightly boozy Gleason let his secret loose with a phrase reminiscent of his Honeymooners days: "We've got'em… aliens!"

THE RISE AND FALL OF THE KNIGHTS TEMPLAR

The Crusades, Christendom's quest to recover and hold the Holy Land, saw the rise of several influential military orders. Of these, the Knights Templar had perhaps the greatest lasting influence—and took the hardest fall.

July 15, 1099: On that day, the First Crusade stormed Jerusalem and slaughtered everyone in sight—Jews, Muslims, Christians—didn't matter. This unleashed a wave of pilgrimage, as European Christians flocked to now-accessible Palestine and its holy sites. Though Jerusalem's loss was a blow to Islam, it was a bonanza for the region's thieves, from Saracens to lapsed Crusaders: a steady stream of naive pilgrims to rob.

DEFENDING THE FAITHFUL

French knight Hugues de Payen, with eight chivalrous comrades, swore to guard the travelers. In 1119, they gathered at the Church of the Holy Sepulchre and pledged their lives to poverty, chastity, and obedience

before King Baldwin II of Jerusalem. The Order of Poor Knights of the Temple of Solomon took up headquarters in said Temple.

GOING MAINSTREAM

The Templars did their work well, and in 1127 Baldwin sent a Templar embassy to Europe to secure a marriage that would ensure the royal succession in Jerusalem. Not only did they succeed, they became rock stars of sorts. Influential nobles showered the Order with money and real estate, the foundation of its future wealth. With this growth came a formal code of rules. Some highlights include:

◆ Templars could not desert the battlefield or leave a castle by stealth.

◆ They had to wear white habits, except for sergeants and squires who could wear black.

◈ They had to tonsure (shave) their crowns and wear beards.

◈ They had to dine in communal silence, broken only by Scriptural readings.

◈ They had to be chaste, except for married men joining with their wives' consent.

A LAW UNTO THEMSELVES—AND NEVER MIND THAT PESKY "POVERTY" PART

Now with offices in Europe to manage the Order's growing assets, the Templars returned to Palestine to join in the Kingdom's ongoing defense. In 1139, Pope Innocent II decreed the Order answerable only to the Holy See. Now exempt from the tithe, the Order was entitled to accept tithes! The Knights Templar had come far.

By the mid-1100s, the Templars had become a church within a church, a nation within a nation, and a major banking concern. Templar keeps were well-defended depositories, and the Order became financiers to the crowned heads of Europe—even to the Papacy. Their reputation for meticulous bookkeeping and secure transactions underpinned Europe's financial markets, even as their soldiers kept fighting for the faith in the Holy Land.

DOWNFALL

Templar prowess notwithstanding, the Crusaders couldn't hold the Holy Land. In 1187, Saladin the Kurd retook Jerusalem, martyring 230 captured Templars. Factional fighting between Christians sped the collapse as the 1200s wore on. In 1291, the last Crusader outpost at Acre fell to the Mamelukes of Egypt. Though the Templars had taken a hosing along with the other Christian forces, their troubles had just begun.

King Philip IV of France owed the Order a lot of money,

and they made him more nervous at home than they did fighting in Palestine. In 1307, Philip ordered the arrest of all Templars in France. They stood accused of apostasy, devil worship, sodomy, desecration, and greed. Hideous torture produced piles of confessions, much like those of the later Inquisition. The Order was looted, shattered, and officially dissolved. In March 1314, Jacques de Molay, the last Grand Master of the Knights Templar, was burned at the stake.

WHITHER THE TEMPLARS?

Many Templar assets passed to the Knights Hospitallers. The Order survived in Portugal as the Order of Christ, where it exists to this day in form similar to British knightly orders. A Templar fleet escaped from La Rochelle and vanished; it may have reached Scotland. Swiss folktales suggest that some Templars took their loot and expertise to Switzerland, possibly laying the groundwork for what would one day become the Swiss banking industry.

DEADLY BLING?: THE CURSE OF THE HOPE DIAMOND

Diamonds are a girl's best friend, a jeweler's meal ticket, and serious status symbols for those who can afford them. But there's one famous diamond whose brilliant color comes with a cloudy history. The Hope Diamond is one of the world's most beautiful gemstones—and one that some say causes death and suffering to those who possess it. So is the Hope Diamond really cursed? There's a lot of evidence that says "no," but there have been some really strange coincidences.

THE ORIGIN OF HOPE

It's believed that this shockingly large, blue-hued diamond came from India several centuries ago. At the time, the exceptional diamond was slightly more than 112 carats, which is enormous. (On average, a diamond in an engagement ring ranges from a quarter to a full carat.) According to legend, a thief stole the diamond from the eye of a Hindu statue, but scholars don't think the shape would have been right to sit in the face of a statue. Nevertheless, the story states that the young thief was torn apart by wild dogs soon after he sold the diamond, making this the first life claimed by the jewel.

COURTS, CARATS, AND CARNAGE

In the mid-1600s, a French jeweler named Tavernier purchased the diamond in India and kept it for several years without incident before selling it to King Louis XIV in 1668, along with several other jewels. The king recut the diamond in 1673, taking it down to 67 carats. This new cut emphasized the jewel's clarity, and Louis liked to wear the "Blue Diamond of the Crown" around his neck on special occasions. He, too, owned the gemstone without much trouble.

More than a hundred years later, France's King Louis XVI possessed the stone. In 1791, when the royal family tried to flee the country, the crown jewels were hidden for safekeeping, but they were stolen the following year. Some were eventually returned, but the blue diamond was not. King Louis XVI and his wife Marie Antoinette died by guillotine in 1793. Those who believe in the curse are eager to include these two romantic figures in the list of cursed owners, but their deaths probably had more to do with the angry mobs of the French Revolution than a piece of jewelry..

RIGHT THIS WAY, MR. HOPE

It is unknown what happened to the big blue diamond from the time it was stolen in France until it appeared in England nearly 50 years later. When the diamond reappeared, it wasn't the same size as before—it was now only about 45 carats. Had it been cut again to disguise its identity? Or was this a new diamond altogether? Because the blue diamond was so unique in color and size, it was believed to be the diamond in question.

In the 1830s, wealthy banker Henry Philip Hope purchased the diamond, henceforth known as the Hope Diamond. When he died (of natural causes) in 1839, he bequeathed the gem to his oldest nephew, and it eventually ended up with the nephew's grandson, Francis Hope.

Francis Hope is the next person supposedly cursed by the diamond. Francis was a notorious gambler and was generally bad with money. Though he owned the diamond, he was not allowed to sell it without his family's permission, which he finally got in 1901 when he announced he was bankrupt. It's doubtful that the diamond had anything to do with Francis's bad luck, though that's what some believers suggest.

COMING TO AMERICA

Joseph Frankel and Sons of New York purchased the diamond from Francis, and by 1909, after a few trades between the world's most notable jewelers, the Hope Diamond found itself in the hands of famous French jeweler Pierre Cartier. That's where rumors of a curse may have actually originated.

Allegedly, Cartier came up with the curse concept in order to sell the diamond to Evalyn Walsh McLean, a rich socialite who claimed that bad luck charms always turned into good luck charms in her hands. Cartier may have embellished the terrible things that had befallen previous owners of his special diamond so that McLean would purchase it—which she did. Cartier even inserted a clause in the sales contract, which stated that if any fatality occurred in the family within six months, the Hope Diamond could be exchanged for jewelry valued at the $180,000 McLean paid for the stone. Nevertheless, McLean wore the diamond on a chain around her neck constantly, and the spookiness surrounding the gem started picking up steam.

Whether or not anything can be blamed on the jewel, it certainly can't be denied that McLean had a pretty miserable life starting around the time she purchased the diamond. Her eldest son died at age nine in a fiery car crash. Years later, her 25-year-old daughter killed herself. Not long after that, her husband was declared insane and was committed to a mental institution for the rest of his life. With rumors swirling about the Hope Diamond's curse, everyone pointed to the necklace when these terrible events took place.

In 1947, when McLean died (while wearing the diamond) at age 60, the Hope Diamond and most of her other treasures were sold to pay off debts. American jeweler Harry Winston forked over the $1 million asking price for McLean's entire jewelry collection.

HOPE ON DISPLAY

If Harry Winston was scared of the alleged curse, he didn't show it. Winston had long wanted to start a collection of gemstones to display for the general public, so in 1958, when the Smithsonian Institute started one in Washington, D.C., he sent the Hope Diamond to them as a centerpiece. These days, it's kept under glass as a central figure for the National Gem Collection at the National

Museum of Natural History. So far, no one's dropped dead from checking it out.

IT'S A BIRD! IT'S A PLANE! IT'S...AVROCAR?!?

Not all UFOs are alien spaceships. One top-secret program was contracted out by the U.S. military to an aircraft company in Canada.

Oh, the 1950s—a time of sock hops, drive-in movies, and the Cold War between America and the Soviet Union, when each superpower waged war against the other in the arenas of scientific technology, astronomy, and politics. It was also a time when discussion of life on other planets was rampant, fueled by the alleged crash of an alien spaceship near Roswell, New Mexico, in 1947.

WATCH THE SKIES

Speculation abounded about the unidentified flying objects (UFOs) spotted nearly every week by everyone from farmers to airplane pilots. As time passed, government authorities began to wonder if the flying saucers were, in fact, part of a secret Russian program to create a new type of air force. Fearful that such a craft would upset the existing balance of power, the U.S. Air Force decided to produce its own saucer-shape ship.

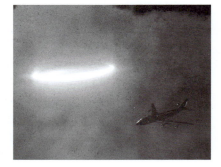

In 1953, the military contacted Avro Aircraft Limited of Canada, an aircraft manufacturing company that operated in Malton, Ontario, between 1945

and 1962. Project Silverbug was initially proposed simply because the government wanted to find out if UFOs could be manufactured by humans. But before long, both the military and the scientific community were speculating about its potential. Intrigued by the idea, designers at Avro—led by British aeronautical engineer John Frost—began working on the VZ-9-AV Avrocar. The round craft would have been right at home in a scene from the classic science fiction film *The Day the Earth Stood Still*. Security for the project was so tight that it probably generated rumors that America was actually testing a captured alien spacecraft—speculation that remains alive and well even today.

OF THIS EARTH

By 1958, the company had produced two prototypes, which were 18 feet in diameter and 3.5 feet tall. Constructed around a large triangle, the Avrocar was shaped like a disk, with a curved upper surface. It included an enclosed 124-blade turbo-rotor at the center of the triangle, which provided lifting power through an opening in the bottom of the craft. The turbo also powered the craft's controls. Although conceived as being able to carry two passengers, in reality a single pilot could barely fit inside the cramped space. The Avrocar was operated with a single control stick, which activated different panels around the ship. Airflow issued from a large center ring, which was controlled by the pilot to guide the craft either vertically or horizontally.

The military envisioned using the craft as "flying Jeeps" that would hover close to the ground and move at a maximum speed of 40 mph. But that, apparently, was only going to be the beginning. Avro had its own plans, which included not just commercial Avrocars, but also a family-size Avrowagon, an Avrotruck for larger loads,

Avroangel to rush people to the hospital, and a military Avropelican, which, like a pelican hunting for fish, would conduct surveillance for submarines.

BUT DOES IT FLY?

The prototypes impressed the U.S. Army enough to award Avro a $2 million contract. Unfortunately, the Avrocar project was canceled when an economic downturn forced the company to temporarily close and restructure. When Avro Aircraft reopened, the original team of designers had dispersed. Further efforts to revive the project were unsuccessful, and repeated testing proved that the craft was inherently unstable. It soon became apparent that whatever UFOs were spotted overhead, it was unlikely that they came from this planet. Project Silverbug was abandoned when funding ran out in March 1961, but one of the two Avrocar prototypes is housed at the U.S. Army Transportation Museum in Fort Eustis, Virginia.

TIME TRAVELERS

Hold on to your hat—you're in for a wild, mind-blowing ride back and forth through the realms of time!

In 2013, many people didn't believe President Obama when he claimed that he often fired guns on the skeet shooting range at Camp David. But others believed that Obama had actually come close to revealing the "real" truth: that he has been working for the CIA for more than 30 years, and that he had personally used the CIA's top secret "jump room" to visit Mars on several occasions as a young man. This is probably not the wildest conspiracy theory about a president that's ever circulated, but it's certainly in the top tier.

However, there's at least one witness who claims to have

known the future president in his Mars-hopping days: a Seattle attorney named Andrew Basiago, who also only claims to have been to Mars himself as an Earth ambassador to a Martian civilization in the early 1980s.

But by then, Basiago says, he was an old hand with the CIA: some years before, when he was only 12, he was a participant in a top secret initiative called Project Pegasus, an elite force that used radiant energy principles discovered in the papers of inventor Nikola Tesla to travel through time.

Basiago claims that he traveled through time using eight different technologies as a boy, but mainly using a teleporter that consisted of two "elliptical booms" that stood eight feet tall, positioned about ten feet apart and separated by a curtain of radiant energy. Participants would jump through the curtain and enter a "vortal tunnel" that took them through time and space. By jumping though, Basiago claims to have attended Ford's Theatre on the night Abraham Lincoln was shot more than once—often enough that on a few occasions, he saw himself, on other trips, among the crowd. Oddly, though this would imply that each "jump" took him to the same "timeline," he says that every time he attended the theatre, the events of the night came off slightly differently, as though he were going to different "timelines" on each trip.

But Lincoln's assassination wasn't the only historic event Basiago claims to have attended. In 1972, he says, he used a "plasma confinement chamber" in East Hanover, New Jersey, to travel back to 1863 to see the Gettysburg Address. Basiago even claims that photographic evidence of this exists; In the foreground of the one photograph of Lincoln at Gettysburg that exists stands a young boy in oversized men's shoes, standing casually outside of the crowd in the background. Basiago says he is the boy.

Basiago told his story over the course of several appearances on *Coast to Coast AM*, a radio program where conspiracies, UFOs, hauntings and other strange phenomena are discussed during late night broadcasts. The online forums on which listeners discuss the topics spoken about on the show once brought forth the story of another alleged time traveler: the story of John Titor, who began posting on the forum in 2000 and claimed to be a time traveler from 2036. Physicists tried to drill him on the mathematics and theories behind time travel, and he seemed to pass every test.

Titor claimed that he was a soldier based in Tampa who was visiting year 2000 for personal reasons—perhaps to collect old family photos that had been destroyed by his time. He even posted schematics showing the devices he used to travel in time, and many at the time became convinced that he was telling the truth.

However, the stories he told about the future of the United States failed to come to pass. In 2001, he claimed that unrest in America surrounding the 2004 presidential election would gradually build up until it became a full-on Civil War, broadly defined as a war between urban and rural parts of the country eventually splitting the United States into five regions. In 2011, he claimed, he was a young teenage soldier for a group called The Fighting Diamondbacks fighting for the rural armies. But the war, he said, would end in 2015 when Russia launched a nuclear assault destroying most American cities, killing as many as half of the people in the country and creating a "new" America in which Omaha, Nebraska, served as the nation's capital. Titor said there was an upside to this: in many ways, he said, the world was better with half of the people gone.

Titor's odd story found a lot of supporters when it was

first posted, and the events of September 11, 2001 convinced many people that World War III was, in fact, at hand. However, the 2004 election came and went without anything happening in the United States that could ever reasonably be called a civil war breaking out. There was still no such war going in 2008, either, by which time Titor claimed that the war would be fully raging and undeniable.

Fans of *Coast to Coast AM* are certainly not the only people who claim to have traveled through time, though, and some of the supposed time travelers have far more bona fide military credentials than Titor, who eventually disappeared from the forums. In 1935, Sir Victor Goddard, an air marshal in the Royal Air Force, claimed that he flew into a strange storm while flying his plane above an airfield in Scotland. The turbulence was so bad that he nearly crashed, and he emerged from the storm to find that the landscape beneath him now contained strange-looking aircraft in hangars that weren't there before, all attended by officers wearing blue uniforms instead of the brown ones the RAF normally used. Four years later, the RAF officially changed the uniforms from brown to blue and began using planes like the ones he had seen after the storm.

This wasn't Goddard's only brush with the unknown. A decade later, he overheard an officer telling of a dream he'd had in which Air Marshall Goddard had died in a wreck when the plane he was flying in iced over and crashed on a beach. That night, Goddard's plane did, indeed, ice over, and an emergency landing was forced on a beach. Though the dream had ended with Goddard dead, Goddard, having had a sort of early warning, kept his cool and brought the plane safely down. The dream he overheard may very well have saved his life.

REBEL WITH A CURSE: JAMES DEAN AND "LITTLE BASTARD"

From the moment James Dean first walked onto a Hollywood set, countless people have emulated his cool style and attitude. When Dean died in a car crash in 1955 at age 24, his iconic status was immortalized. Perhaps this is partly due to the strange details that surrounded his death. Did a cursed car take the rising star away before his time?

HOW MUCH IS THAT PORSCHE IN THE WINDOW?

In 1955, heartthrob James Dean purchased a silver Porsche 550 Spyder, which he nicknamed "Little Bastard." Dean painted the number 130 on the hood and the car's saucy name on the back.

On the morning of September 30, Dean drove the Porsche to his mechanic for a quick tune-up before heading to a race he was planning to enter. The car checked out, and Dean left, making plans to meet up with a few friends and a *Life* magazine photographer later that day.

Everyone who knew Dean knew he liked to drive fast. The movie star set out on the highway, driving at top speeds in his beloved Porsche. He actually got stopped for speeding at one point but got back on the road after getting a ticket.

But when the sun got in his eyes and another car made a quick left turn, Dean couldn't stop in time. Screeching brakes, twisted metal, and an ambulance that couldn't make it to the hospital in time signaled the end of James Dean's short life.

YOU NEED BRAKE PADS, A NEW ALTERNATOR, AND A PRIEST

Within a year or so of Dean's fatal car crash, his Porsche was involved in a number of unusual—and sometimes deadly—incidents. Were they all coincidental, or was the car actually cursed? Consider the following:

❖ Two doctors claimed several of Little Bastard's parts. One of the docs was killed and the other seriously injured in separate accidents. Someone else purchased the tires, which blew simultaneously, sending their new owner to the hospital.

❖ The Fresno garage where the car was kept for a while after Dean's death was the site of a major fire. The California State Highway Patrol removed the car from Fresno, figuring they could show the charred remains of Dean's car to warn teenagers about the dangers of careless driving. When the vehicle transporting the remains of the car crashed en route to the site, the driver was thrown from his vehicle and died.

❖ The display the Highway Patrol produced was incredibly popular, of course, but it also turned out to be dangerous. The legs of a young boy looking at the car were crushed when three of the cables holding the vehicle upright suddenly broke, bringing the heavy metal down onto the boy's body. When the car left the exhibit, it broke in half on the truck used to haul it away and killed a worker involved in the loading process.

❖ In 1959, there was another attempt to display the car. Though it was welded together, legend has it that the car suddenly broke into 11 pieces. The following year, the owner had finally had enough and decided to have the Porsche shipped from Miami back to California. Little Bastard was loaded onto a sealed boxcar, but when the train arrived in L.A., the car was gone. Thieves may have taken the car, sure, but there were reports that the boxcar hadn't been disturbed. Whether or not the car was cursed, with all the trouble it caused, perhaps it was for the best that it finally disappeared.

THE MYSTERIOUS 27 CLUB

If you're a rock star approaching your 27th birthday, perhaps you should take a year-long hiatus. The curse known as the 27 Club is a relatively new one, but that doesn't make it any less freaky. For those about to blow out 27 candles, good luck...

FOUNDING MEMBERS

Keith Richards and Eric Clapton both cite guitarist Robert Johnson as a major musical influence. Born on May 8, 1911, Johnson played guitar so well at such a young age that some said he must have made a deal with the devil. Those spooky speculations have survived in part due

to Johnson's untimely death. The blues guitar legend died on August 16, 1938, at age 27, after the husband of a woman Johnson was involved with allegedly poisoned him.

After Johnson, the next rocker to join the 27 Club was Brian Jones, one of the founding members of the Rolling Stones. Jones was a lifelong asthma sufferer, so his descent into drug and alcohol addiction was probably not the wisest choice. Still, the sex and drugs inherent in the music biz proved to be too much for Jones to pass up. Some believe he committed suicide because his time with the Stones had recently come to an end. Due to his enlarged liver, autopsy reports led others to believe he overdosed. Either way, when Jones's body was found lifeless in a swimming pool in 1969, the British Invasion rocker was dead at age 27. Jones, another person who cited Johnson as a musical influence, was unfortunately following in his idol's footsteps—and he would soon have company.

A TRIO OF INDUCTEES

About a year later, the 27 Club would claim its biggest star yet. The counterculture of the late 1960s had embraced the incredibly talented Jimi Hendrix. Legions of fans worshipped the man and his music and sang along to "Purple Haze" at Woodstock. On September 18, 1970, the rock star—who, like so many before him and since, had an affinity for drugs and alcohol—died in London

at age 27. Hendrix aspirated on his own vomit after taking too many sleeping pills.

Texas-born singer-songwriter Janis Joplin was another megastar at the time and a friend of Jimi. Largely regarded as one of the most influential artists in American history, Joplin's gravelly voice and vocal stylings were unique and incredibly popular. She screeched, growled, and strutted through numbers like "Me and Bobby McGee" and "Piece of My Heart." She also tended to play as hard as she worked, typically with the aid of drugs (including psychedelics and methamphetamines) and her signature drink, Southern Comfort whiskey.

On October 4, 1970, when Joplin failed to show up for a recording session for her upcoming album *Pearl*, one of her managers got worried and went to her motel room to check on her. He found the singer dead—at age 27—from a heroin overdose. After Joplin's death, rumors about this strange and tragic "club" began to take hold in the superstitious minds of the general public. Another tragic death less than a year later didn't help.

Florida-born Jim Morrison was yet another hard-living, super famous, devil-may-care rock star. He skyrocketed to fame as the front man for the 1960s band The Doors. The young musician was known for his roguish good looks, his dark, curly hair, and his charismatic and mysterious attitude. But his fans didn't have much time to love him. The Doors hit their peak in the late 1960s, and Morrison died (at age 27) from an overdose on July 3, 1971.

THE LATEST INDUCTEE

If you were a fan of rock 'n' roll music in 1994 (especially if you were younger than 30), you probably remember where you were when you heard that Kurt Cobain had died. The tormented lead singer of the incredibly popular alternative rock band Nirvana had committed suicide after a lifelong battle with drug addiction, chronic pain, and debilitating depression.

At the tender age of (you guessed it) 27, Cobain had ended his life and had become the most recent member of the 27 Club. Cobain seemed to have known about the "elite" group of young, dead rock musicians: His mother told reporters, "Now he's gone and joined that stupid club. I told him not to join that stupid club."

ROCK STEADY? PROBABLY NOT

It is odd that these incredibly influential, iconic figures in music would all die before their time and all at age 27. However, when you think about all of the other rock stars who didn't die—Keith Richards, Iggy Pop, and Ozzy Osbourne, to name a few—the odds don't seem so bad. Plus, when you consider how hard these individuals have lived their lives, it seems extraordinary that they have lived as long as they have.

Rock musicians are shrouded in speculation and the all-powerful effects of idol worship, so it's no wonder that fans have elevated what's probably just a strange coincidence into the stuff of legend or curse. Whether you believe in the 27 Club or not, you can still rock out to the music these tragic stars left behind.

CHAPTER 6
ENIGMATIC PEOPLE & CULTURES

THE ANASAZI

WHO WERE THE ANASAZI?

Across the deserts and mesas of the region known as the Four Corners, where Arizona, New Mexico, Colorado, and Utah meet, backcountry hikers and motoring tourists can easily spot reminders of an ancient people. From the towering stone structures at Chaco Culture National Historical Park to cliff dwellings at Mesa Verde National Park to the ubiquitous scatters of broken pottery and stone tools, these remains tell the story of a culture that spread out across the arid Southwest during ancient times. The Anasazi are believed to have lived in the region from about AD 1 through AD 1300 (though the exact beginning of the culture is difficult to determine because there is no particular defining event). In their everyday lives, they created black-on-white pottery styles that distinguish subregions within the culture, traded with neighboring cultures (including those to the south in Central America), and built ceremonial structures called kivas, which were used for religious or communal purposes.

THE EXODUS EXPLAINED

Spanish conquistadors exploring the Southwest noted the abandoned cliff dwellings and ruined plazas, and archaeologists today still try to understand what might have caused the Anasazi to move from their homes and villages throughout the region. Over time, researchers have posed a number of theories, including the idea that the Anasazi were driven from their villages by hostile nomads, such as those from the Apache or Ute tribes. Others believe that the Anasazi fought among themselves, causing a drastic reduction in their populations, and a few extraterrestrial-minded theorists have suggested that the Anasazi civilization was destroyed by aliens. Today, the prevalent hypothesis among scientists is that a long-term drought affected the area, destroying agricultural fields and forcing people to abandon their largest villages. Scientists and archaeologists have worked together to reconstruct the region's climate data and compare it with material that has been excavated. Based on their findings, many agree that some combination of environmental and cultural factors caused the dispersal of the Anasazi from the large-scale ruins seen throughout the landscape today.

THEIR JOURNEY

Although many writers—of fiction and nonfiction alike—romanticize the Anasazi as a people who mysteriously disappeared from the region, they did not actually disappear. Those living in large ancient villages and cultural centers did indeed disperse, but the people themselves did not simply disappear. Today, descendents of the Anasazi can be found living throughout New Mexico and Arizona. The Hopi tribe in northern Arizona, as well as those living in approximately 20 pueblos in New Mexico, are the modern-day descendants of the Anasazi. The

Pueblos in New Mexico whose modern inhabitants consider the Anasazi their ancestors include: Acoma, Cochiti, Isleta, Jemez, Laguna, Nambe, Picuris, Pojoaque, San Felipe, San Ildefonso, Ohkay Owingeh (formerly referred to as San Juan), Sandia, Santa Ana, Santa Clara, Santo Domingo, Taos, Tesuque, Zia, and Zuni.

THE MOUND BUILDERS: MYTHMAKING IN EARLY AMERICA

The search for an improbable past, or, how to make a mountain out of a molehill.

In the early 1840s, the fledgling United States was gripped by a controversy that spilled from the parlors of the educated men in Boston and Philadelphia—the core of the nation's intellectual elite—onto the pages of the newspapers printed for mass edification. In the tiny farming village of Grave Creek, Virginia (now West Virginia), on the banks of the Ohio River stood one of the largest earthen mounds discovered during white man's progress westward. The existence of these mounds, spread liberally throughout the Mississippi Valley, Ohio River Valley, and much of the southeast, was commonly known and had caused a great deal of speculative excite-

ment since Europeans had first arrived on the continent. Hernando de Soto, for one, had mentioned the mounds of the Southeast during his wandering in that region.

MONEY WELL SPENT

The colonists who settled the East Coast noticed that the mounds, which came in a variety of sizes and shapes, were typically placed near excellent sites for villages and farms. The Grave Creek mound was among the first of the major earthworks discovered by white men in their westward expansion. By 1838, the property was owned and farmed by the Tomlinson family. Abelard B. Tomlinson took an interest in the mound on his family's land and decided to open a vertical shaft from its summit, 70 feet high, to the center. He discovered skeletal remains at various levels and a timbered vault at the base containing the remains of two individuals. More importantly, he discovered a sandstone tablet inscribed with three lines of characters of unknown origin

WHO WERE THE MOUND BUILDERS?

Owing to the general belief that the aborigines were lazy and incapable of such large, earth-moving operations and the fact that none of the tribes who dwelt near the mounds claimed any knowledge of who had built them, many 19th-century Americans believed that the mound builders could not have been the ancestors of the Native American tribes they encountered. Wild and fantastic stories arose, and by the early 19th century, the average American assumed that the mound builders had been a pre-Columbian expedition from the Old World—Vikings, Israelites, refugees from Atlantis—all these and more had their champions. Most agreed, however, that the New World had once hosted and given rise to a civilization as advanced as that of the Aztecs and Incas who had then fallen into disarray or been conquered by the savage barbarians that now inhabited the land. Speculation on the history of the mound builders led many, including Thomas Jefferson, to visit mounds and conduct their own studies.

MORMONS AND THE MOUNDS

Meanwhile, the Grave Creek tablet fanned the flames of a controversy that was roaring over the newly established Church of Jesus Christ of Latter Day Saints, founded by Joseph Smith. The Mormon religion is based upon the belief that the American continent was once inhabited by lost tribes of Israel who divided into warring factions and fought each other to near extinction. The last surviving prophet of these people, Mormon, inscribed his people's history upon gold tablets, which were interred in a mound near present-day Palmyra, New York, until they were revealed to fifteen-year-old Joseph Smith in 1823. Though many Americans were ready to believe that the mounds represented the remains of a nonaboriginal culture, they were less ready to believe in Smith's new religion. Smith and his adherents were persecuted horribly, and Smith was killed by an angry mob while leading his followers west. Critics of the Saints (as the Mormons prefer to be called) point to the early 19th-century publication of several popular and well distributed books purporting that the earthen mounds of North America were the remains of lost tribes of Israel. These texts claimed that evidence would eventually be discovered to support their author's assertions. That the young Smith should have his revelation so soon after these fanciful studies were published struck many observers as entirely too coincidental. Thus, Abelard Tomlinson's excavation of the sandstone tablet with its strange figures ignited the passions of both Smith's followers and his detractors.

ENTER THE SCHOLAR

Into this theological, and ultimately anthropological, maelstrom strode Henry Rowe Schoolcraft, a mineralogist whose keen interest in Native American history had led to his appointment as head of Indian affairs. While working in Sault Ste. Marie, Schoolcraft married a native woman and mastered the Ojibwa language. Schoolcraft traveled to Grave Creek to examine Tomlinson's tablet and concluded that the figures were indeed a language but deferred to more learned scholars to determine just which language they represented. The opinions were many and varied—from Celtic runes to early Greek; experts the world over weighed in with their opinions. Nevertheless, Schoolcraft was more concerned with physical evidence and close study of the mounds themselves, and he remained convinced that the mounds and the artifacts they carried were the products of ancestors of the Native Americans. Schoolcraft's theory flew in the face of both those who sought to defend and those who sought to debunk the Mormon belief, and it would be more than three decades until serious scholarship and the emergence of true archeological techniques began to shift opinion on the subject.

ANSWERS PROPOSED, BUT QUESTIONS STILL ABOUND

History has vindicated Schoolcraft's careful and thoughtful study of the mounds. Today, we know that the mound builders were not descendants of Israel, nor were they the offspring of Vikings. They were simply the ancient and more numerous predecessors of the Native Americans, who constructed the mounds for protection from floods and as burial sites, temples, and defense strongholds. As for the Grave Creek tablet: Scholars today generally agree that the figures are not a written language but simply a fanciful design whose meaning, if ever there was one, has been lost to the ages. Though the Smithsonian Institute has several etchings of the tablet in its collection, the whereabouts of the actual tablet have disappeared in the expanding frontier of history.

IDENTITIES LOST:
THE DRUIDS AND THE PICTS

What do you know about the Druids? How about the Picts? Chances are, what you know (or think you know) is wrong. These two "lost" peoples are saddled with serious cases of mistaken identity.

Most contemporary perceptions of the Druids and Picts tend to be derived from legend and lore. As such, our conceptions of these peoples range from erroneous and unlikely to just plain foolish.

Let's start with the Druids. They are often credited with the building of Stonehenge, the great stone megalith believed to be their sacred temple, as well as their arena for savage human sacrifice rituals. True or False?

False. First of all, Stonehenge was built around 2000 BC— 1,400 years before the Druids emerged. Second, though we know admittedly little of Druidic practice, it seemed to be traditional and conservative. The Druids did have specific divinity-related beliefs, but it is not known whether they actually carried out human sacrifices.

What about the Picts? Although often reduced to a mythical race of magical fairies, the Picts actually ruled Scotland before the Scots. So who were the Druids and the Picts?

THE DRUIDS—THE PRIESTLY CLASS

As the priestly class of Celtic society, the Druids served as the Celts' spiritual leaders—repositories of knowledge about the world and the universe, as well as authorities on Celtic history, law, religion, and culture. In short, they were the preservers of the Celtic way of life.

The Druids provided the Celts with a connection to their

gods, the universe, and the natural order. They preached of the power and authority of the deities and taught the immortality of the soul and reincarnation. They were experts in astronomy and the natural world. They also had an innate connection to all things living: They preferred holding great rituals among natural shrines provided by the forests, springs, and groves.

To become a Druid, one had to survive extensive training. Druid wannabes and Druid-trained minstrels and bards had to endure as many as 20 years of oral education and memorization.

MORE POWERFUL THAN CELTIC CHIEFTAINS

In terms of power, the Druids took a backseat to no one. Even the Celtic chieftains, well-versed in power politics, recognized the overarching authority of the Druids. Celtic society had well-defined power and social structures and territories and property rights. The Druids were deemed the ultimate arbiters in all matters relating to such. If there was a legal or financial dispute between two parties, it was unequivocally settled in special Druid-presided courts. Armed conflicts were immediately ended by Druid rulings. Their word was final.

In the end, however, there were two forces to which even the Druids had to succumb—the Romans and Christianity. With the Roman invasion of Britain in AD 43, Emperor Claudius decreed that Druidism throughout the Roman Empire was to be outlawed. The Romans destroyed the last vestiges of official Druidism in Britain with the annihilation of the Druid stronghold of Anglesey in AD 61. Surviving Druids fled to unconquered Ireland and Scotland, only to become completely marginalized by the influence of Christianity within a few centuries.

Stripped of power and status, the Druids of ancient Celtic society disappeared. They morphed into wandering poets and storytellers with no connection to their once illustrious past.

THE PICTS—THE PAINTED PEOPLE

The Picts were, in simplest terms, the people who inhabited ancient Scotland before the Scots. Their origins are unknown, but some scholars believe that the Picts were descendants of the Caledonians or other Iron Age tribes who invaded Britain.

No one knows what the Picts called themselves; the origin of their name comes from other sources and probably derives from the Pictish custom of tattooing or painting their bodies. The Irish called them Cruithni, meaning "the people of the designs." The Romans called them Picti, which is Latin for "painted people"; however, the Romans probably used the term as a general moniker for all the untamed peoples living north of Hadrian's Wall.

A SECOND-HAND HISTORY

The Picts themselves left no written records. All descriptions of their history and culture come from second-hand accounts. The earliest of these is a Roman account from AD 297 stating that the Picti and the Hiberni (Irish) were already well-established enemies of the Britons to the south.

The Picts were also well-established enemies of each other. Before the arrival of the Romans, the Picts spent most of their time fighting amongst themselves. The threat posed by the Roman conquest of Britain forced the squabbling Pict kingdoms to come together and eventually evolve into the nation-state of Pictland. The united Picts were strong enough not only to resist conquest by the Romans, but also to launch periodic raids on Roman-occupied Britain.

Having defied the Romans, the Picts later succumbed to a more benevolent invasion launched by Irish Christian missionaries. Arriving in Pictland in the late 6th century, they succeeded in converting the polytheistic Pict elite within two decades. Much of the written history of the Picts comes from the Irish Christian annals. If not for the writings of the Romans and the Irish missionaries, we might not have knowledge of the Picts today.

Despite the existence of an established Pict state, Pictland disappeared with the changing of its name to the Kingdom of Alba in AD 843, a move signifying the rise of the Gaels as the dominant people in Scotland. By the 11th century, virtually all vestiges of them had vanished.

NOSTRADAMUS: SEER OF VISIONS

Nostradamus was born in December 1503 in Saint-Rémy-de-Provence, a small town in southern France. Little is known about his childhood except that he came from a very large family and that he may have been educated by his maternal great-grandfather. In his teens, Nostradamus entered the University of Avignon but was only there for about a year before the school was forced to close its doors due

to an outbreak of the plague. He later became a successful apothecary and even created a pill that could supposedly protect against the plague.

LOOKING TO THE FUTURE

It is believed that some time in the 1540s, Nostradamus began taking an interest in the occult, particularly in ways to predict the future. His preferred method was scrying: gazing into a bowl of water or a mirror and waiting for visions to appear.

Nostradamus published a highly successful almanac for the year 1550, which included some of his prophecies and predictions. This almanac was so successful that Nostradamus wrote more, perhaps even several a year, until his death in 1566. Even so, it was a single book that caused the most controversy, both when it was released and even today.

LES PROPHÉTIES

In addition to creating his almanacs, Nostradamus also began compiling his previously unpublished prophecies into one massive volume. Released in 1555, *Les Prophéties* (*The Prophecies*) would become one of the most controversial and perplexing books ever written. The book contained hundreds of quatrains (four-line stanzas or poems), but Nostradamus worried that some might see his prophecies as demonic, so he encoded them to obscure their true meanings. To do this, Nostradamus did everything from playing with the syntax of the

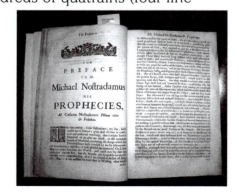

quatrains to switching between French, Greek, Latin, and other languages.

When first released, some people did think that Nostradamus was in league with the devil. Others simply thought he was insane and that his quatrains were nothing more than the ramblings of a delusional man. As time went on, though, people started looking to Nostradamus's prophecies to see if they were coming true. It became a common practice that after a major event in history, people would pull out a copy of *Les Prophéties* to see if they could find a hidden reference to it buried in one of Nostradamus's quatrains. It is a practice that has continued to this day and only gets more and more common as the years go by.

LOST IN TRANSLATION

One of the interesting and frustrating things about Nostradamus's *Les Prophéties* is that due to the printing procedures in his time, no two editions of his book were ever alike. Not only were there differences in spelling or punctuation, but entire words and phrases were often changed, especially when translated from French to English. Presently, there are more than 200 editions of *Les Prophéties* in print, all of which have subtle differences in the text. So it's not surprising that people from all over the world have looked into their version and found references to the French Revolution, Napoleon, the rise of Hitler, the JFK assassination, even the Apollo moon landing. But of all the messages reportedly hidden in Nostradamus's quatrains, the most talked about recently are those relating to the terrorist attacks on September 11, 2001.

Soon after the Twin Towers fell, an e-mail started making the rounds, which claimed that Nostradamus had predicted the events and quoted the following quatrain as proof:

> *In the City of God there will be a great thunder,*
>
> *Two Brothers torn apart by Chaos,*
>
> *While the fortress endures,*
>
> *The great leader will succumb,*
>
> *The third big war will begin when the big city is burning*
>
> —*Nostradamus, 1654*

Anyone reading the above can clearly see that Nostradamus is describing September 11, the Twin Towers ("Two Brothers") falling, and the start of World War III. Pretty chilling, except Nostradamus never wrote it. It's nothing more than an internet hoax that spread like wildfire. It's a pretty bad hoax, too. First, Nostradamus wrote quatrains, which have four lines. This one has five. Also, consider that the date Nostradamus supposedly penned this—1654—was almost 90 years after he died. Nostradamus might have been able to see the future, but there's no mention of him being able to write from beyond the grave.

However, others believe Nostradamus did indeed pen a quatrain that predicted September 11. It is quatrain I.87, which when translated reads:

> *Volcanic fire from the center of the earth*
>
> *Will cause tremors around the new city;*
>
> *Two great rocks will make war for a long time*
>
> *Then Arethusa will redden a new river.*

Those who believe this quatrain predicted September 11 believe that the "new city" is a thinly-veiled reference to New York City. They further state that Nostradamus would often use rocks to refer to religious beliefs and that the third line refers to the religious differences between the United States and the terrorists. Skeptic James Randi, however, believes that the "new city" referred to is Naples, not New York. So who's right? No one is really sure, so for now, the debate continues…at least until the next major catastrophe hits and people go scrambling to the bookshelves to see what Nostradamus had to say about it.

RASPUTIN: MANIPULATOR OR MALIGNED HOLY MAN?

We know this much: Grigori Yefimovich Rasputin, a barely literate Russian peasant, grew close to the last tsaritsa—close enough to cost him his life. Incredibly lurid stories ricocheted off the walls of the Winter Palace: drunken satyr, faith healer, master manipulator. What's true? And why does Rasputin fascinate us even today?

The Rasputin saga began on January 22, 1869, in the

grubby peasant village of Pokrovskoe, Russia. Baby Rasputin was born on the day of the Orthodox saint Grigori, and was thus named after him. There wasn't much to distinguish little Grigori from tens of millions of Russian peasant kids, and he grew up a rowdy drunk. He married a peasant woman named Praskovia, who hung back in Pokrovskoe raising their five kids in Rasputin's general absence.

At 28, Rasputin was born again, rural Russian style. He sobered up—a small miracle in itself—and wandered between monasteries seeking knowledge. Evidently, he fell in with the khlysti—a secretive, heretical Eastern Orthodox sect swirling with rumors of orgies, flagellation, and the like. He gained a mystical aura, and his behavior reflected a sincere spiritual search.

In 1903, he wandered to the capital, St. Petersburg, where he impressed the local Orthodox clergy. Word spread. The ruling Romanov family soon heard of Rasputin.

The Romanovs held a powerful yet precarious position. Ethnically, they were more German than Russian, a hot-button topic for the bona fide Slavs they ruled. Greedy flatterers and brutal infighters made the corridors of power a steep slope with weak rock and loose mud: As you climbed, your prestige and influence grew—but woe to you if you slipped (or were pushed). In that event, the rest would step aside and let you fall—caring only to get out of your way. This was no safe place for a naive peasant—however spiritually inclined. Even the Romanovs lived in fear, for tsars tended to die violent deaths. They ruled a dirt-poor population that was seething with resentment. Tsaryevich ("tsar's son") Alexei, the heir apparent, was a fragile hemophiliac who could bleed out from a skinned knee, aptly symbolic of the blood in the political water in St. Petersburg in those final days of the last tsar, Nikolai II.

As the tsaritsa worried over gravely ill Alexei in 1906, she thought of Rasputin and his healing reputation. He answered her summons in person, blessed Alexei with an Orthodox icon and left. Alexei improved, and Tsaritsa Aleksandra was hooked on Rasputin. She consulted him often, promoted him to her friends, and pulled him onto that treacherous slope of imperial favor. For his final ten years, Rasputin became a polarizing figure as he grew more influential. His small covey of upper-crest supporters (mostly female) hung on his every word, even as a growing legion of nobles, peasants, and clergy saw in Rasputin all that was wrong with the monarchy.

What few ask now is: What was Rasputin thinking? What was he feeling? His swift rise from muddy fields to the royal palace gave him an understandable ego trip. He was a peasant but not an idiot; he realized his rise would earn him jealous enemies. The sheer fury of their hatred seems to have surprised, frightened, and saddened him, for he wasn't a hateful man. He certainly felt duty-bound to the tsaritsa, whose unwavering favor deflected most of his enemies' blows. Rasputin's internal spiritual struggle (against sin, toward holiness) registers authentic, at least until his last year or so of life—but he made regular visits to prostitutes long before that. Defenders claim that he was only steeling himself against sexual temptation; you can imagine what his enemies said.

Life worsened for Rasputin in 1914, when he was stabbed by a former prostitute. He survived, but the experience shook him. After recuperating, he abandoned any restraint he'd ever exercised. Rasputin better acquainted himself with the bottoms of liquor bottles—and those of his visitors. Most likely he expected death and gave in to natural human desires: Cartoons portrayed him as a cancer infecting the monarchy, especially after Russia went to war with Germany. Military setbacks left Russians with much to mourn and resent. A wave of mandatory patriotism swept Russia, focusing discontent upon the royal family's Germanic ties.

In the end, clergy and nobility agreed with the media: down with Rasputin.

Led by a fabulously rich libertine named Felix Yusupov, a group of Rasputin's enemies lured him to a meeting on December 29, 1916. The popular story is that he scarfed a bunch of poisoned food and wine, somehow didn't die, was shot, got up, was beaten and shot some more, then was finally tied up and thrown alive through the ice of a frozen river. What is sure: Rasputin was shot, bound, and dumped into freezing water to die. Whether or not he was still alive when dumped and whether or not he actually partook of the cyanide munchies, he was found with at least one fatal bullet wound.

The tsaritsa buried her advisor on royal property. After the Romanovs fell, a mob dug up Rasputin and burned his corpse. To our knowledge, nothing remains of him.

Rasputin had predicted that if he were slain by the nobility, the Russian monarchy wouldn't long survive him. His prophecy came true: Less than a year after his death, the Russian Revolution deposed the tsar. The Reds would soon murder the entire royal family; had they captured Rasputin, it's hard to imagine him being spared. For the "Mad Monk" who was neither mad nor monastic, the muddy road of life had dead-ended in the treacherous forest of imperial favor.

DEMONIZED BY MYTHOLOGY: LUCREZIA BORGIA

In public perception, she rates alongside Jezebel and Messalina for conniving promiscuity. But who was the real Lucrezia Borgia, and how depraved was she?

BACKDROP

Lucrezia Borgia's life was orchestrated by the intense political and military competition of the Italian Renaissance. Italy was a gaggle of city-states and noble families, with foreign neighbors butting in, all jostling for advantage in a sleazy multiplayer chess game of shifting alliances, fiefdom grants, political marriages, excommunication, and warfare. The Vatican sat at that chessboard, and Lucrezia was a pawn.

THE BORGIA FAMILY

Lucrezia's father was Cardinal Rodrigo Borgia, later Pope Alexander VI, the poster boy for corrupt, lascivious popes. His Holiness fathered Lucrezia and her three brothers with a mistress; her most prominent brother, Cesare, was ambitious and ruthless even by the inflated standards of the Renaissance. Lucrezia had the misfortune of being born into a family whose name evoked fear and loathing, with good cause.

LUCREZIA'S MARITAL CAREER

When Lucrezia reached the age of 13 in 1493, her father married her off to Giovanni Sforza to cement an alliance with Sforza's powerful Milanese clan, thus boosting Cesare's fortunes. When Alexander no longer needed to make nice with the Sforzas, he had Lucrezia's marriage to Giovanni annulled.

It was rumored that Lucrezia had a love affair and bore a son out of wedlock. In 1498, she entered an arranged marriage to Alfonso of Bisceglie, this time to ingratiate Cesare with the king of Naples. When that notion soured, "unknown assailants" (probably her brother Cesare's henchmen) assassinated Alfonso. Lucrezia had grown to love her husband, and she went into a deep depression.

In 1501, Alexander brokered Lucrezia's marital hand to Alfonso d'Este, Prince of Ferrara. The new bride's sister-in-law, Isabella, delighted in snubs and snippy comments, but Lucrezia now knew the game. While keeping up appearances as a noble, dutiful Ferrarese matron, she carried on with Isabella's husband. After the deaths of Alexander (1503) and then Cesare (1507), Lucrezia could finally settle down. She died on June 24, 1519, at the age of 39, of complications from childbirth.

HEINOUS ALLEGATIONS

Detractors love to paint Lucrezia as a Renaissance floozy with a poison-filled ring who had incestuous relations with her father and brother. It makes lurid reading, but the sliver of truth in such allegations is rather dull and tame. She did have lovers between marriages and outside of wedlock, as did many in her time. Living as a political pawn, can anyone blame her for wanting romantic flings? It would be peculiar if she hadn't.

There's no evidence supporting the incest slander—but there is good reason to reject it. Unlike her father and Cesare, Lucrezia had authentic religious scruples. Her consent would be unthinkable. She remained fond of each unto his death and mourned both. Would she have lamented those who'd traumatized her? Her later life is inconsistent with childhood molestation: She adjusted well, had a healthy love life when she could, and was never self-destructive.

THE ORIGINS OF SLURS

Some aspersions were bandied during her life, mainly as weapons against the Borgias, spurred by Cesare's atrocious conduct. In 1833, Victor Hugo wrote a play that painted Lucrezia as a princess of poison, reveling in each toxic takedown. This, not actual history, has adhered to the public perception. It libels a pleasant, loving woman whose fortunes were dictated mainly by men of great power and limitless greed.

JACK THE RIPPER

Between 1888 and 1891, he brutally murdered at least five women in London's East End. But was there really a connection between Jack the Ripper and the British royal family?

The serial killer known as Jack the Ripper is one of history's most famous murderers. He breathed terror into the gas-lit streets and foggy back alleys of the Whitechapel area of London and became renowned the world over. Despite the countless books and movies detailing his story, however, his identity and motives remain shrouded in mystery. One of the most popular theories, espoused by the 2001 movie *From Hell* (starring Johnny Depp), links the killer to the British royal family.

THE CRIMES

Five murders are definitively attributed to Jack the Ripper, and he has variously been connected to at least six other unsolved slayings in the London area. The body of the first victim, 43-year-old Mary Ann Nichols, was discovered on the morning of August 31, 1888. Nichols's throat had been cut and her abdomen mutilated. The subsequent murders, which took place over a three-year period, grew in brutality. The killer removed the uterus of his second victim, Annie Chapman; part of the womb and left kidney of Catherine Eddowes; and the heart of Mary Kelly. All of his victims were prostitutes.

THE NAME

A man claiming to be the murderer sent a letter (dated September 25, 1888) to the Central News Agency, which passed it on to the Metropolitan Police. The letter included the line, "I am down on whores and I shant quit ripping them till I do get buckled." It was signed, "Yours truly, Jack the Ripper." A later postcard included the same sign-off. When police went public with details of the letters, the name "Jack the Ripper" stuck.

THE SUSPECTS

Officers from the Metropolitan Police and Scotland Yard had four main suspects: a poor Polish resident of Whitechapel by the name of Kosminski, a barrister who committed suicide in December 1888, a Russian-born thief, and an American doctor who fled to the States in November 1888 while on bail for gross indecency. Since there was little or no evidence against any of these men, the case spawned many conspiracy theories, the most popular of which links the killings to the royal family.

THE ROYAL CONSPIRACY

The heir to the British throne was Prince Albert Victor, grandson of Queen Victoria and son of the man who would later become King Edward VII. The prince, popularly known as Eddy, had a penchant for hanging around in the East End, and rumors abounded that he had a daughter, Alice, out of wedlock with a shop girl named Annie Crook. To prevent major embarrassment to the Crown, Eddy sought assistance from Queen Victoria's physician, Dr. William Gull, who institutionalized Annie to keep her quiet. However, her friends, including Mary Kelly, also knew the identity of Alice's father, so Dr. Gull created the persona of Jack the Ripper and brutally silenced them one by one. A variation on this theory has Dr. Gull acting without the knowledge of

the prince, instead driven by madness resulting from a stroke he suffered in 1887.

Royal involvement would certainly explain why the police were unable to uncover the identity of the Ripper or to even settle on a prime suspect. There was a shop girl named Annie Crook who had an illegitimate daughter named Alice, but there is nothing to connect her to either the prince or the murdered prostitutes. In fact, there is no evidence to suggest that the murdered women knew one another. Until the identity of Jack the Ripper is settled beyond doubt, these and other conspiracy theories will likely persist.

WHO WAS DAVY CROCKETT?

Just who exactly was Davy Crockett? Was he a rough-and-tumble pioneer, a man whose fearless exploits helped tame the wilderness? Or was he an ambitious and self-promoting politician, made famous by a well-orchestrated public relations campaign and a little help from Hollywood?

A MAN FROM TENNESSEE

Some aspects of David "Davy" Crockett's life are not in dispute, though much of it is. We know that he was born on August 17, 1786, in eastern Tennessee. His first wife was Mary "Polly" Finley, who died in 1815. He soon remarried, taking the widow Elizabeth Patton to be his bride.

Crockett was an excellent hunter. Often his rifle enabled him to provide food for his wife and five children. But he wasn't entirely an outdoorsman: He was elected to the Tennessee legislature in 1821, then the United States House of Representatives in 1827. For the next decade he was in and out of Congress, and when he found himself in a hard-fought battle for the Congressional seat in 1835, he threatened that if he lost the election he would tell his constituents "to go to hell" and move to Texas. He lost the vote and kept his word, departing to Texas, where he met his end at the Alamo on March 6, 1836.

TWO MEN THE SAME—TWO MEN DIFFERENT

Crockett is always lumped together with Daniel Boone as one of the two premier American frontiersmen, blazing trails through untamed wilderness. Without question, Boone was the real deal. He explored Kentucky when it was populated almost primarily by Native Americans, built the Wilderness Road to provide greater access to the region, led settlers into Kentucky when it was just a howling wilderness, and narrowly escaped death numerous times.

Crockett's life followed a different path. Bitten by the political bug upon his first foray into elected office, he progressed from justice of the peace to U.S. Congressman in a remarkably short time, particularly because political campaigns then—as now—cost money, and Crockett's low-budget campaigns would have embarrassed a shoestring.

Crockett was a natural for politics. Independent-minded and loyal to his backwoods constituents, he was also gregarious, quick-witted, and personable. Once, a flock of guinea hens showed up at an outside political debate and squawked so loudly that his opponent was completely unnerved. Crockett, however, joked that the birds had actually been chanting "Crockett, Crockett, Crockett," which is why the other candidate was spooked. He won the debate and the election.

Contrast that with the stoic and reclusive Boone, who probably would have preferred to swim the entire length of the Mississippi River rather than hobnob and glad-hand. As one story has it, Boone once welcomed a visitor to his cabin and in conversation asked where the man lived. When informed that he resided about 70 miles from Boone's home, Boone turned to his wife and said, "Old woman, we must move, they are crowding us."

A LION WITH A TOUCH OF AIRTH-QUAKE

Crockett enjoyed his reputation as a humble backwoods-man in sophisticated Washington, D.C. This reputation was spread even further by the wildly popular 1831 play *The Lion of the West*. The main character, obviously based on Crockett, is a Congressman from Kentucky named Nimrod Wildfire, who boasts that he's "half horse, half alligator, a touch of the airth-quake, with a sprinkling of the steamboat." Beginning in 1835, with the publication of the so-called *Crockett Almanacs*, he was portrayed in an even more sensational light—as biographer Mark Derr calls him, a "comic Hercules."

Thanks to Walt Disney in the mid-1950s, Crockett became one of the first media sensations of the modern age. By the time Disney was finished with his legend, people everywhere were singing about Tennessee mountaintops and wearing coonskin caps (which Crockett never wore). From then on, Crockett's image as an authentic American hero was set.

A LITTLE OF THIS, A LITTLE OF THAT

So who was Davy Crockett? Like all of us, he's hard to pin down—a combination of different factors that make a characterization difficult. Part frontiersman and part politician mixed with a keen wit, unabashed honesty, and a friendly nature, Davy Crockett in the end was 100 percent uniquely American.

THE STORY OF THE TASADAY

A 1972 National Geographic *article announced the discovery of a gentle, pristine Stone Age people in the Philippines: the Tasaday. Skeptics say the Tasaday were a hoax perpetrated by the Marcos government—but are they right?*

In 1971, strongman Ferdinand Marcos was dictator of the Philippines. His wealthy crony, Manuel Elizalde, Jr., was head of Panamin, a minority-rights watchdog agency. In a nation with 7,107 islands, 12 major regional languages, and hundreds of ethnic groups, such an agency has its work cut out for it.

THE DISCOVERY

The Philippines' second largest island, Mindanao, is bigger than Maine, with lots of jungle. According to Elizalde, a western Mindanao tribesman put him in contact with the Tasaday. The tribe numbered only a couple dozen and lived amid primitive conditions. Their language bore relation to nearby tongues but lacked words for war and violence. They seemed to be living in gentle simplicity, marveling at Elizalde as a deity and protector. For his part, Elizalde clamped the full power of the Philippine state into place to shield his newfound people.

One of the few study groups permitted to examine the

Tasaday was from *National Geographic*, which introduced the Tasaday to the world in 1972.

After Marcos fell from power in 1986, investigators studying the lives of the Tasaday revealed that it was all a fraud. According to reports, Elizalde had recruited the Tasaday from long-established local tribes and forced them to role-play a Stone Age lifestyle. The Tasaday eventually became the "Tasaday Hoax."

A SCAM REVEALED?

A couple of Tasaday told a sad story: They normally farmed nearby, living in huts rather than caves, but Elizalde made them wear loincloths and do dog-and-pony shows for paying visitors. The poorer and more primitive they looked, the more money they would get. In one instance, a group of German journalists who set out to document the Tasaday found them dressed primitively— sort of. They were wearing leaves, but they had stuck them onto their clothing, which was visible beneath the foliage. Scientific skepticism soon surfaced as well: How could they have remained that isolated for so long, even on Mindanao? Why didn't modern disease now decimate them? Why did their tools show evidence of steel-knife manufacturing?

Elizalde didn't back down easily. In an attempt to keep up the charade, he flew a few Tasaday to Manila to sue the naysayers for libel. With Marcos ousted, however, Elizalde was less able to influence investigators or control what they had access to. Eminent linguist Lawrence Reid decided that the Tasaday were indeed an offshoot of a regional tribe—but one that had been living in the area for only 150 years, not more than a thousand as was claimed. Likely as confused as everyone else at this point, previous Tasaday whistleblowers now confessed that translators had bribed them to say the whole thing was a hoax.

THE AFTERMATH

Elizalde later fled to Costa Rica, squandered his money, and died a drug addict. If he had indeed fabricated the history of the Tasaday, what was his motivation? It could have been a public-relations ploy, because the Marcos government had a well-earned reputation for repression. A strong minority-rights stance in defense of the Tasaday could be expected to buff some tarnish off the government's image. Commerce likely played a role, for the Tasaday episode denied huge tracts of jungle to logging interests. Perhaps those interests hadn't played ball with Marcos and/or Elizalde.

LYING IN WAIT

There are those who are famous in life, and there are those who are more famous in death—and "Eugene" is certainly the latter. An unclaimed body in the town of Sabina, Ohio, turned a funeral home into a tourist attraction and drew visitors from far and wide.

When most people die, their remains are quickly taken care of. Not so for the mystery man known as Eugene. After being embalmed, he hung around for nearly 35 years before finally being laid to rest.

Eugene's decades-long saga began and ended in the tiny town of Sabina, about ten miles outside of Wilmington, where he died along the 3C highway on June 6, 1929. Several people reported seeing him walk listlessly through town, as if he were ill, but he didn't stop or ask for help.

A MAN WITHOUT A NAME

No identification was found on his body except for a slip of paper containing an address in Cincinnati. But when the Cincinnati police went to investigate, they found only a vacant lot. Police talked to a man living next door named Eugene Johnson, and thus did the unknown dead man get the moniker Eugene.

All that is known about Eugene is that he was African American, was thought to be between 50 and 80 years old, and died of natural causes. Authorities took him to the Littleton Funeral Home, where he was embalmed. But rather than bury Eugene in a pauper's grave, the funeral home's owners decided to wait on the off chance that his survivors might be located.

ON DISPLAY

Eugene spent the next three and a half decades at the Littleton Funeral Home, lying in state in a small house in the side yard. As his legend grew, curiosity seekers started dropping by to see the man that no one knew— so many, in fact, that the owners erected a screen across the room to protect him from grabby souvenir seekers. Out of respect, the funeral home provided Eugene with a brand-new suit every year.

Before long, Eugene had become a bona fide tourist attraction. Buses passing through town would stop by the funeral home so travelers could stretch their legs and take a peek at the "Sabina mummy." On holidays and summer weekends, a line of people waiting to pass by Eugene's resting place would form, which only proves how hungry the citizens of Sabina were for entertainment on a Saturday night.

During the 35 years that Eugene lay in state, an estimated one and a half million people paid their respects—while a million of them, including several celebrities, signed his voluminous guest books. Sadly, none of the visitors ever claimed to recognize him.

Eugene sometimes became the victim of pranksters during his years at the Littleton Funeral Home. On a number of occasions he was kidnapped but quickly recovered. Once, members of a fraternity drove him all the way to the Ohio State campus in Columbus.

RESTING IN PEACE

In 1964, Eugene was finally put to rest. It was evident that no one was going to claim him, and many found the pranks being played on him demeaning and harmful to business. Rather than bury Eugene in a potter's field, the owners of the funeral home purchased a plot in Sabina Cemetery and paid for his burial expenses.

Only a handful of people attended the service for Eugene on October 21, and employees of the Sabina Cemetery, Spurgeon Vault Company, and Littleton Funeral Home acted as pallbearers. A local Methodist minister offered a few words and a prayer, and Eugene was—finally—able to rest in peace.

THE CLAIRVOYANT CRIME-BUSTER

Before there were TV shows like Ghost Whisperer *and* Medium, *which make the idea of solving crimes through ESP seem almost commonplace, there was psychic detective Arthur Price Roberts. And his work was accomplished in the early 1900s, when high-tech aids like electronic surveillance and DNA identification were still only far-fetched dreams. Police in those times often used psychics to help solve many cases.*

"I SEE DEAD PEOPLE"

A modest man born in Wales in 1866, Roberts deliberately avoided a formal education because he believed too much learning could stifle his unusual abilities. He moved to Milwaukee, Wisconsin, as a young man where, ironically, the man who never learned to read was nicknamed "Doc."

One of his earliest well-known cases involved a baffling missing person incident in Peshtigo, a small town about 160 miles north of Milwaukee. A man named Duncan McGregor had gone missing in July 1905, leaving no clue as to his whereabouts. The police searched for him for months, and finally his desperate wife decided to go to the psychic detective who had already made a name for himself in Milwaukee. She didn't even have to explain the situation to Roberts; he knew immediately upon meeting her who she was.

Roberts meditated on the vanished husband, then sadly had to tell Mrs. McGregor that he'd been murdered and that his body was in the Peshtigo River, caught near the bottom in a pile of timber. Roberts proved correct in every detail.

MYSTERY OF THE MAD BOMBERS

Roberts solved numerous documented cases. He helped a Chicago man find his brother who had traveled to Albuquerque and had not been heard from for months; Roberts predicted that the brother's body would be found in a certain spot in Devil's Canyon, and it was.

After coming up with new evidence for an 11th hour pardon, Roberts saved a Chicago man named Ignatz Potz, who had been condemned to die for a murder he didn't commit. But his most famous coup came in 1935 when he correctly predicted that the city of Milwaukee would be hit by six large dynamite explosions, losing a town hall, banks, and police stations. People snickered; such mayhem was unheard of in Milwaukee. Roberts made his prediction on October 18 of that year. In little more than a week, the Milwaukee area entered a time of terror.

First, a town hall in the outlying community of Shorewood was blasted, killing two children and wounding many other people. A few weeks later, the mad bombers hit two banks and two police stations. Federal agents descended upon the city, and several local officers were assigned to work solely on solving the bombings. Finally, the police went to Roberts to learn what was coming next. Roberts told them one more blast was in the works, that it would be south of the Menomonee River, and that it would be the final bomb. Police took him at his word and blanketed the area with officers and sharpshooters. And sure enough, on November 4, a garage in the predicted area blew to smithereens in an explosion that could be heard as far as eight miles away. The two terrorists, young men 18 and 21 years old, had been hard at work in the shed assembling 50 pounds of dynamite when their plan literally backfired. Few people argued with Roberts's abilities after that.

HIS FINAL FORTUNE

Roberts's eeriest prediction, however, may have been that of his own death. In November 1939, he told a group of assembled friends that he would be leaving this world on January 2, 1940. And he did, passing quietly in his own home on that exact date. Many of his most amazing accomplishments will probably never be known because a lot of his work was done secretly for various law enforcement agencies. But "Doc" Roberts had an undeniable gift, and he died secure in the knowledge that he had used it to help others as best he could.

THE KUANO RIVER BOY

Around the world, feral (or wild) children have reportedly been raised by wolves, monkeys, and even ostriches, but a boy seen splashing about the banks of a river in northern India in the 1970s was rumored to have been raised by fish or lizards.

FROM THE BLACK LAGOON

The boy, about 15 years old when first discovered in 1973 by residents of the small town of Baragdava, had blackish-green skin and no hair. His head appeared malformed in a strange bullet shape, and he was entirely naked. "Lizard people" complete with green scales have been reported from time to time around the world, but this boy lacked scales, gills, or even webbed toes.

He lived amid the crocodiles in the Kuano River without fear of attack and was able to hold his breath and stay underwater longer than thought humanly possible. But strangest of all, hundreds of people, including police and reporters, saw him run across the surface of the water. This may have been explained by the slightly submerged dam surface. A person dashing across it might have appeared to be running on water to observers at a distance. Either way, there was no question that the boy was strangely at home in the river habitat..

SON OF A WATER SPIRIT

Although his initial appearance was a shock, a village woman named Somni, who found the boy lying in a field one day, noticed a birthmark on his back that was identical to that of the infant son she had lost in the swirling river several years earlier. Somni even had an explanation for why her son, whom she'd named Ramchandra, ended up as a "merman." Somni claimed that she had been raped and impregnated by a giant water spirit during a rainstorm. Villagers accepted Somni's story; however, her husband displayed the same bullet-shape skull as the River Boy.

THE AMPHIBIOUS LIFE

Although Ramchandra, if that was indeed his true identity, preferred to remain in the river most of the time, he did seem curious about the human villagers living nearby and would sometimes approach them. Several times he was captured and brought to the village by force. He enjoyed eating vegetables left for him along the riverbank, although his main sustenance came from raw fish and frogs that he gulped from the river without using his hands.

NOT EASY BEING GREEN

For nine years, the River Boy interacted with the villagers of Baragdava, but eventually he came to a terrible end. In 1982, after two policemen tried to catch him, he made an escape from what had been his home village and swam to another river town about 12 miles away.

There he approached a woman tending a small tea shop. The woman was so frightened by his naked, greenish appearance that she doused him with a pan of boiling water. Ramchandra ran back to the river where he died from severe burns. His body was eventually retrieved floating on the water. The Kuano River Boy's age at the time of his tragic death was estimated at 24.

The River Boy's green-tinted skin was never definitively explained, although it was presumed to have been from long-time contact with the river water and perhaps algae. But strangely, there are records of other green children of unknown origin. In 1887, some field workers observed a boy and a girl as they timidly emerged from a cave in Banjos, Spain. The skin of both children was bright green, and they wore clothing made from an unrecognizable fabric. They spoke a language no one understood, but when the girl learned some Spanish, she told the villagers that a whirlwind had brought them to the cave from another land where the sun was never seen. Both children perished young—the boy after some days and the girl after about five years—but their skin turned a paler and paler green the longer they were out of the cave.

CHAPTER 7

UNEXPLAINED PHENOMENA

ARE YOU GOING TO EAT THAT JESUS?

Images of religious icons, particularly Jesus and the Virgin Mary, sometimes show up in the oddest places. Some people believe they are divine. What's the story?

Sightings of religious symbols or images, called religious simulacra, in unexpected places are common enough that they've become incorporated into pop culture. Many of the people who discover or are involved in these sightings consider them to be miraculous events. Some also claim that the objects in which the images appear have special properties, such as bringing good luck or being immune to the ravages of time.

JESUS AND MARY

For Christians, Jesus and the Virgin Mary are among the most significant religious figures, and not coincidentally, they also seem to make the most common appearances—often in food. Perhaps the quintessential sighting of a Christian religious symbol in food occurred in 1978, when a New Mexico woman named Maria Rubio was making a burrito. She noticed that a burn on the tortilla appeared to be in the shape of Jesus' head. After receiving the blessing of a priest, she built a shrine to house the tortilla.

ISLAMIC WORDS

Not surprisingly, religious sightings do not always involve Christian figures or symbols. In the Islamic world, the perception of the Arabic word for Allah roughly parallels the sighting of Jesus, the Virgin Mary, or other religious figures by Christians. Similarly, the objects involved sometimes have mystical properties ascribed to them. In 2006, a Kazakh farmer discovered an egg that villagers claimed had the name of Allah on its shell. After the sighting was verified by the local mosque, Bites Amantayeva, the farmer who discovered the egg, decided to keep it, saying, "We don't think it'll go bad." The name of Allah has also been sighted on fish scales, on beans, and in tomato slices.

SELLING SIMULACRA

Sightings of religious images can have commercial as well as spiritual implications. In 1996, someone at a coffee shop in Nashville, Tennessee, discovered a cinnamon bun that bore a striking resemblance to Mother Teresa. The coffee shop parlayed the discovery into a line of merchandise, including coffee mugs and T-shirts. The merchandise was marketed with a NunBun trademark after Mother Teresa asked the shop to stop using the phrase "Immaculate Confection."

The proliferation of internet auction sites such as eBay has created a market for these "miraculous" objects. One of the widest-known auctions occurred in 2004, when a Florida woman named Diane Duyser auctioned part of a grilled cheese sandwich she claimed bore the image of the Virgin Mary on eBay. Duyser asserted that the sandwich, which she had been storing since it was made in 1994, had never grown moldy and had brought her good luck, allowing her to win $70,000 at a casino. The sandwich was eventually purchased by another casino for $28,000.

Religious sightings—especially if they have been contrived somehow—are not always viewed in a positive light. In 1997, Nike produced several models of basketball shoes that unintentionally featured a logo that, when viewed from right to left, resembled the Arabic word for Allah. The Council on American-Islamic Relations (CAIR) quickly demanded an apology, and Nike had little choice but to recall the shoes. The settlement between Nike and CAIR also included Arabic training for Nike graphic designers and Nike-built playgrounds in Muslim communities.

A SCIENTIFIC EXPLANATION?

While the parties involved in sightings of religious symbols often consider them to be miraculous in nature, the prevailing scientific view is that, rather than miraculous, they are occurrences of pareidolia, a psychological phenomenon in which random stimuli are interpreted as being meaningful in some way. As part of its intellectual process, the mind tries to make sense of what may be unrelated images. This is the same phenomenon that psychologists credit with forming the likeness of a man in the moon or shapes in clouds. It's also what's involved when the brain creates pictures from the famous Rorschach inkblots.

A VOICE FROM BEYOND THE GRAVE

◇◇◇

After the murder of Teresita Basa in the late 1970s, another woman began to speak in Basa's voice—saying things that only Teresita could have known—to help solve the mystery of her murder.

In February 1977, firemen broke into a burning apartment on North Pine Grove Avenue in Chicago. Beneath a pile of burning clothes, they found the naked body of 47-year-old Teresita Basa, a hospital worker who was said to be a member of the Filipino aristocracy. There were bruises on her neck and a kitchen knife was embedded in her chest. Her body was in a position that caused the police to suspect that she had been raped.

However, an autopsy revealed that she hadn't been raped; in fact, she was a virgin. Police were left without a single lead: They had no suspects and no apparent motive for the brutal murder. The solution would come from the strangest of all possible sources—a voice from beyond the grave.

"I AM TERESITA BASA"

In the nearby suburb of Evanston, shortly after Teresita's death, Remibios Chua started going into trances during which she spoke in Tagalog in a slow, clear voice that said, "I am Teresita Basa." Although Remibios had worked at the same hospital as Teresita, they worked different shifts, and the only time they are known to have even crossed paths was during a new-employee orientation. Remibios's husband, Dr. Jose Chua, had never heard of Basa.

While speaking in Teresita's voice, Remibios's accent changed, and when she awoke from the trances, she remembered very little, if anything, about what she had said. However, while speaking in the mysterious voice, she claimed that Teresita's killer was Allan Showery, an employee at the hospital where both women had worked. She also stated that he had killed her while stealing jewelry for rent money.

Through Remibios's lips, the voice pleaded for them to contact the police. The frightened couple initially resisted, fearing that the authorities would think that they should be locked away. But when the voice returned and continued pleading for an investigation, the Chuas finally contacted the Evanston police, who put them in touch with Joe Stachula, a criminal investigator for the Chicago Police Department.

Lacking any other clues, Stachula interviewed the Chuas. During their conversation, Remibios not only named the killer, but she also told Stachula exactly where to find the jewelry that Showery had allegedly stolen from Teresita. Prior to that, the police were not even aware that anything had been taken from the apartment.

Remarkably, when police began investigating Showery, they found his girlfriend in possession of Teresita's jewelry. Although the authorities declined to list the voice from beyond the grave as evidence, Showery was arrested, and he initially confessed to the crime. When his lawyers learned that information leading to his arrest had come from supernatural sources, they advised him to recant his confession.

THE SURPRISE CONFESSION

Not surprisingly, the voice became a focal point of the case when it went to trial in January 1979. The defense called the Chuas to the witness stand in an effort to prove that the entire case against Showery was based on remarks made by a woman who claimed to be possessed—hardly the sort of evidence that would hold up in court.

But the prosecution argued that no matter the origin of the voice, it had turned out to be correct. In his closing remarks, prosecuting attorney Thomas Organ said, "Did Teresita Basa come back from the dead and name Showery? I don't know. I'm a skeptic, but it doesn't matter as to guilt or innocence. What does matter is that the information furnished to police checked out. The jewelry was found where the voice said it would be found, and Showery confessed."

Detective Stachula was asked if he believed the Chuas: "I would not call anyone a liar," he said, "Dr. and Mrs. Chua are educated, intelligent people...I listened and acted on what they told me...[and] the case was wrapped up within three hours."

Showery told the jury that he was "just kidding" when he confessed to the crime; he also claimed that the police had coerced him into an admission of guilt. Nevertheless, after 13 hours of deliberation, the jury reported that they were hopelessly deadlocked and a mistrial was declared.

A few weeks later, in a shocking development, Allan Showery changed his plea to "guilty" and was eventually sentenced to 14 years in prison. Some say that Teresita's ghost had visited him and frightened him into confessing.

Obviously shaken by the experience, the Chuas avoided the press as much as possible. In 1980, in her only interview with the press, Remibios noted that during the trial, people were afraid to ride in cars with her, but she said that she was never afraid because the voice said that God would protect her family. Still, she hoped that she would never have to go through such an experience again. "I've done my job," she said. "I don't think I will ever want to go through this same ordeal."

Having attracted national attention, the case quickly became the subject of a best-selling book and countless magazine articles, a TV movie, and a 1990 episode of *Unsolved Mysteries*. The case is often cited as "proof" of psychic phenomena, possession, and ghosts, but it's simply another mystery of the paranormal world. Exactly what it proves is impossible to say; after all, the ghost of Teresita Basa is no longer talking

THE KECKSBURG INCIDENT

Did visitors from outer space once land in a western Pennsylvania thicket?

DROPPING IN FOR A VISIT

On December 9, 1965, an unidentified flying object (UFO) streaked through the late-afternoon sky and landed in Kecksburg—a rural Pennsylvania community about 40 miles southeast of Pittsburgh. This much is not disputed. However, specific accounts vary widely from person to person. Even after closely examining the facts, many people remain undecided about exactly what happened. "Roswell" type incidents—ultra-mysterious in nature and reeking of a governmental cover-up—have an uncanny way of causing confusion.

TRAJECTORY-INTERRUPTUS

A meteor on a collision course with Earth will generally "bounce" as it enters the atmosphere. This occurs due to friction, which forcefully slows the average space rock from 6 to 45 miles per second to a few hundred miles per hour, the speed at which it strikes Earth and officially becomes a meteorite. According to the official explanation offered by the U.S. Air Force, it was a meteorite that landed in Kecksburg. However, witnesses reported

that the object completed back and forth maneuvers before landing at a very low speed—moves that an unpowered chunk of earthbound rock simply cannot perform. Strike one against the meteor theory.

AN ACORN-SHAPE METEORITE?

When a meteor manages to pierce Earth's atmosphere, it has the physical properties of exactly what it is: a space rock. That is to say, it will generally be unevenly shaped, rough, and darkish in color, much like rocks found on Earth. But at Kecksburg, eyewitnesses reported seeing something far, far different. The unusual object they described was bronze to golden in color, acorn-shape, and as large as a Volkswagen Beetle automobile. Unless the universe has started to produce uniformly shaped and colored meteorites, the official explanation seems highly unlikely. Strike two for the meteor theory.

MARKEDLY DIFFERENT

Then there's the baffling issue of markings. A meteorite can be chock-full of holes, cracks, and other such surface imperfections. It can also vary somewhat in color. But it should never, ever have markings that seem intelligently designed. Witnesses at Kecksburg describe intricate writings similar to Egyptian hieroglyphics located near the base of the object. A cursory examination of space rocks at any natural history museum reveals that such a thing doesn't occur naturally. Strike three for the meteor theory. Logically following such a trail, could an unnatural force have been responsible for the item witnessed at Kecksburg? At least one man thought so.

REPORTIS RIGOR MORTIS

Just after the Kecksburg UFO landed, reporter John Murphy arrived at the scene. Like any seasoned pro, the newsman immediately snapped photos and gathered eyewitness accounts of the event. Strangely, FBI agents arrived, cordoned off the area, and confiscated all but one roll of his film. Undaunted, Murphy assembled a radio documentary entitled *Object in the Woods* to describe his experience. Just before the special was to air, the reporter received an unexpected visit by two men. According to a fellow employee, a dark-suited pair identified themselves as government agents and subsequently confiscated a portion of Murphy's audiotapes. A week later, a clearly perturbed Murphy aired a watered-down version of his documentary. In it, he claimed that certain interviewees requested their accounts be removed for fear of retribution at the hands of police, military, and government officials. In 1969, John Murphy was struck dead by an unidentified car while crossing the street.

RESURRECTED BY ROBERT STACK

In all likelihood the Kecksburg incident would have remained dormant and under-explored had it not been for the television show *Unsolved Mysteries*. In a 1990 segment, narrator Robert Stack took an in-depth look at what occurred in Kecksburg, feeding a firestorm of interest that eventually brought forth two new witnesses. The first, a U.S. Air Force officer stationed at Lockbourne AFB (near Columbus, Ohio), claimed to have seen a flatbed truck carrying a mysterious object as it arrived on base on December 10, 1965. The military man told of a tarpaulin-covered conical object that he couldn't identify and a "shoot to kill" order given to him for anyone who ventured too close. He was told that the truck was bound for Wright–Patterson AFB in Dayton, Ohio, an installation that's alleged to contain downed flying saucers. The other witness was a building contractor who claimed to have delivered 6,500 special bricks to a hanger inside Wright–Patterson AFB on December 12, 1965. Curious, he peeked inside the hanger and saw a "bell-shaped" device, 12-feet high, surrounded by several men wearing anti-radiation style suits. Upon leaving, he was told that he had just witnessed an object that would become "common knowledge" in the next 20 years.

WILL WE EVER KNOW THE TRUTH?

Like Roswell before it, we will probably never know for certain what occurred in western Pennsylvania back in 1965. The more that's learned about the case, the more confusing and contradictory it becomes. For instance, the official 1965 meteorite explanation contains more holes than Bonnie and Clyde's death car, and other explanations, such as orbiting space debris (from past U.S. and Russian missions) reentering Earth's atmosphere, seem equally preposterous. In 2005, as the result of a new investigation launched by the Sci-Fi Television Network, NASA asserted that the object was a Russian satellite. According to a NASA spokesperson, documents of this investigation were somehow misplaced in the 1990s. Mysteriously, this finding directly contradicts the official Air Force version that nothing at all was found at the Kecksburg site. It also runs counter to a 2003 report made by NASA's own Nicholas L. Johnson, Chief Scientist for Orbital Debris. That document shows no missing satellites at the time of the incident. This includes a missing Russian Venus Probe (since accounted for)—the very item that was once considered a prime crash candidate.

BRAVE NEW WORLD

These days, visitors to Kecksburg will be hard-pressed to find any trace of the encounter—perhaps that's how it should be. Since speculation comes to an abrupt halt whenever a concrete answer is provided, Kecksburg's reputation as "Roswell of the East" looks secure, at least for the foreseeable future. But if one longs for proof that something mysterious occurred there, they need look no further than the backyard of the Kecksburg Volunteer Fire Department. There, in all of its acorn-shape glory, stands a full-scale mock-up of the spacecraft reportedly found in this peaceful town on December 9, 1965. There too rests the mystery, intrigue, and romance that have accompanied this alleged space traveler for more than 40 years.

STRANGE LIGHTS IN MARFA

According to a 2007 poll, approximately 14 percent of Americans believe they've seen a UFO. How many of them have been in Marfa, Texas?

If anyone is near Marfa at night, they should watch for odd, vivid lights over nearby Mitchell Flat. Many people believe that the lights from UFOs or even alien entities can be seen. The famous Marfa Lights are about the size of basketballs and are usually white, orange, red, or yellow. These unexplained lights only appear at night and usually hover above the ground at about shoulder height. Some of the lights—alone or in pairs—drift and fly around the landscape.

From cowboys to truck drivers, people traveling in Texas near the intersection of U.S. Route 90 and U.S. Route 67 in southwest Texas have reported the Marfa Lights. And these baffling lights don't just appear on the ground. Pilots and airline passengers claim to have seen the Marfa Lights from the skies. So far, no one has proved a natural explanation for the floating orbs.

EYEWITNESS INFORMATION

Two 1988 reports were especially graphic. Pilot R. Weidig was about 8,000 feet above Marfa when he saw the lights and estimated them rising several hundred feet above the ground. Passenger E. Halsell described the lights as larger than the plane and noted that they were pulsating. In 2002, pilot B. Eubanks provided a similar report.

In addition to what can be seen, the Marfa Lights may also trigger low-frequency electromagnetic (radio) waves—which can be heard on special receivers—similar to the "whistlers" caused by lightning. However, unlike such waves from power lines and electrical storms, the Marfa whistlers are extremely loud. They can be heard as the orbs appear, and then they fade when the lights do.

A LITTLE BIT ABOUT MARFA

Marfa is about 60 miles north of the Mexican border and about 190 miles southeast of El Paso. This small, friendly Texas town is 4,800 feet above sea level and covers 1.6 square miles.

In 1883, Marfa was a railroad water stop. It received its name from the wife of the president of the Texas and New Orleans Railroad, who chose the name from a Russian novel that she was reading. A strong argument can be made that this was Dostoyevsky's *The Brothers Karamazov*. The town grew slowly, reaching its peak during World War II when the U.S. government located a prisoner of war camp, the Marfa Army Airfield, and a chemical warfare brigade nearby. (Some skeptics suggest that discarded chemicals may be causing the Marfa Lights, but searchers have found no evidence of such.)

Today, Marfa is home to about 2,500 people. The small town is an emerging arts center with more than a dozen artists' studios and art galleries. However, Marfa remains most famous for its light display. The annual Marfa Lights Festival is one of the town's biggest events, but the mysterious lights attract visitors year-round.

The Marfa Lights are seen almost every clear night, but they never manifest during the daytime. The lights appear between Marfa and nearby Paisano Pass, with the Chinati Mountains as a backdrop.

WIDESPREAD SIGHTINGS

The first documented sighting was by 16-year-old cowhand Robert Reed Ellison during an 1883 cattle drive.

Seeing an odd light in the area, Ellison thought he'd seen an Apache campfire. When he told his story in town, however, settlers told him that they'd seen lights in the area, too, and they'd never found evidence of campfires.

Two years later, 38-year-old Joe Humphreys and his wife, Sally, also reported unexplained lights at Marfa. In 1919, cowboys on a cattle drive paused to search the area for the origin of the lights. Like the others, they found no explanation for what they had seen.

In 1943, the Marfa Lights came to national attention when Fritz Kahl, an airman at the Marfa Army Base, reported that airmen were seeing lights that they couldn't explain. Four years later, he attempted to fly after them in a plane but came up empty again.

EXPLANATIONS?

Some skeptics claim that the lights are headlights from U.S. 67, dismissing the many reports from before cars— or U.S. 67—were in the Marfa area. Others insist that the lights are swamp gas, ball lightning, reflections off mica deposits, or a nightly mirage.

At the other extreme, a contingent of people believe that the floating orbs are friendly observers of life on Earth. For example, Mrs. W. T. Giddings described her father's early 20th-century encounter with the Marfa Lights. He'd become lost during a blizzard, and according to his daughter, the lights "spoke" to him and led him to a cave where he found shelter.

Most studies of the phenomenon, however, conclude that the lights are indeed real but cannot be explained. The 1989 TV show *Unsolved Mysteries* set up equipment to find an explanation. Scientists on the scene could only comment that the lights were not made by people.

SHARE THE WEALTH

Marfa is the most famous location for "ghost lights" and "mystery lights," but it's not the only place to see them. Here are just a few of the legendary unexplained lights that attract visitors to dark roads in Texas on murky nights.

❖ In southeast Texas, a single orb appears regularly near Saratoga on Bragg Road.

❖ The Anson Light appears near Mt. Hope Cemetery in Anson, by U.S. Highway 180.

❖ Since 1850, "Brit Bailey's Light" glows five miles west of Angleton near Highway 35 in Brazoria County.

❖ In January 2008, Stephenville attracted international attention when unexplained lights—and perhaps a metallic spaceship—flew fast and low over the town.

The Marfa Lights appear over Mitchell Flat, which is entirely private property. However, the curious can view the lights from a Texas Highway Department roadside parking area about nine miles east of Marfa on U.S. Highway 90. Seekers should arrive before dusk for the best location, especially during bluebonnet season (mid-April through late May), because this is a popular tourist stop.

The Marfa Lights Festival takes place during Labor Day weekend each year. This annual celebration of Marfa's mystery includes a parade, arts and crafts booths, great food, and a street dance.

MAGNETIC HILL PHENOMENON

It has taken researchers hundreds of years to finally solve the mystery of magnetic hills, or spook hills, as they're often called. This phenomenon, found all over the world, describes places where objects—including cars in neutral gear—move uphill on a slightly sloping road, seemingly defying gravity.

Moncton, in New Brunswick, Canada, lays claim to one of the more famous magnetic hills, called, appropriately, Magnetic Hill. Over the years, it has also been called Fool's Hill and Magic Hill. Since the location made headlines in 1931, hundreds of thousands of tourists have flocked there to witness this phenomenon for themselves.

GO FIGURE

Much to the dismay of paranormal believers, people in science once assumed that a magnetic anomaly caused this event. But advanced physics has concluded this phenomenon is due "to the visual anchoring of the sloping surface to a gravity-relative eye level whose perceived direction is biased by sloping surroundings." In nonscientific jargon, all that says is that it's an optical illusion.

Papers published in the journal of the Association of Psychological Science supported this conclusion based on a series of experiments done with models. They found that if the horizon cannot be seen or is not level then people may be fooled by objects that they expect to be vertical but aren't. False perspective is also a culprit; think, for example, of a line of poles on the horizon that seem to get larger or smaller depending on distance.

Engineers with plumb lines, one made of iron and one made of stone, demonstrated that a slope appearing to go uphill might in reality be going downhill. A good topographical map may also be sufficient to show which way the land is really sloping.

I KNOW A PLACE

Other notable magnetic hills can be found in Wisconsin, Pennsylvania, California, Florida, Barbados, Scotland, Australia, Italy, Greece, and South Korea.

THE PHILIP PHENOMENON: CREATING A GHOST OUT OF THIN AIR

Which came first: the ghost or the séance? That's the million-dollar question regarding the Philip Phenomenon—an astonishing experiment that successfully conjured up a spirit. The only problem is that this ghost never really lived...Or did it?

It all began in 1972, when members of the Toronto Society for Psychical Research (TSPR) conducted an experiment to determine if they could "create" a ghost and study how the power of suggestion affected the results. They wanted to know if they could work with a totally fictitious character—a man they invented from scratch—and somehow make contact with its spirit. And they did.

Dr. A.R.G. Owen, the organization's chief parapsychology researcher, gathered a group of eight people who were interested in the paranormal but had no psychic abilities of their own. The Owen Group, as it was called, was made up of people from all walks of life, including Owen's wife, an accountant, an industrial designer, a former MENSA chairwoman, a housewife, a student, and a bookkeeper. Dr. Joel Whitton, a psychologist, was also present at many of the meetings as an observer.

THE MAKING OF A GHOST

The first order of business was to create the ghost, giving it physical characteristics and a complete background story. According to Dr. Owen, it was important to the study that the spirit be totally made-up, with no strong ties to any historical figure. The group named the ghost Philip and proceeded to bring him to life—on paper, that is. A sketch artist even drew a picture of Philip as the group imagined him. Here is his story:

Philip Aylesford was an aristocratic Englishman who was born in 1624. As a supporter of the King, he was knighted at age 16 and went on to make a name for himself in the military. He married Dorothea, the beautiful daughter of a nobleman who lived nearby. Unfortunately, Dorothea's appearance was deceiving, as her personality was cold and unyielding. As a Catholic, Philip wouldn't divorce his wife, so he found escape by riding around the grounds of his estate. One day, he came across a gypsy camp. There, he found true love in the arms of the raven-haired Margo, whose dark eyes seemed to look into his soul. He brought her to Diddington Manor, his family home, and hid her in the gatehouse near the stable. But it wasn't meant to be: Dorothea soon discovered her husband's secret affair and retaliated by accusing the gypsy woman of stealing and practicing witchcraft. Afraid of damaging his own reputation, Philip did not step forward in Margo's defense, and she was burned at the stake.

After the death of his beloved, Philip was tormented with guilt and loneliness; he killed himself in 1654 at age 30.

FOCUS, FOCUS, FOCUS

In September 1972, after the tale was written, the group began meeting regularly. Reports of these meetings vary. Some accounts describe them as mere gatherings in which group members would discuss Philip and meditate on the details of his life. With no results after about a year, the group moved on to a more traditional method of communing with ghosts: holding séances in a darkened room, sitting around a table with appropriate music and objects that might have been used by Philip or his family. Another version has the group beginning with séances and switching to the more casual setting later. The setting itself is ultimately secondary to the results: Through the focus and concentration of the group, Philip soon began to make his presence known. He answered questions by tapping on the table for "yes" or "no." Just to be sure, a "yes" tap confirmed that he was, indeed, Philip.

A PHYSICAL PRESENCE

After communication was established, the Philip Phenomenon took on a life of its own. Through the tapping, Philip was able to answer questions about the details of his life. He was also able to correctly answer questions about people and places of that historical time period, although these were all facts that were familiar to at least one member of the group. Philip even seemed to develop a personality, exuding emotions that changed the atmosphere of the entire room. But most amazingly, he was able to exhibit some remarkable physical manifestations, such as making objects move, turning lights on and off at the group's request, and performing incredible feats with the table: It shifted, it danced on one leg, and it even moved across the room.

In order to demonstrate the results of this experiment, the group held a séance in front of an audience of 50 people; the session was also videotaped. Philip rose to the occasion—and so did the table. In addition to tapping on the table and manipulating the lights, Philip made the entire table levitate half an inch off the ground!

The experiment was deemed a success, as there was little doubt that something paranormal was occurring during the sessions. However, the Owen Group never actually realized its original goal of getting the ghost of Philip to materialize. But the TSPR did go on to re-create the experiment successfully on several other occasions with a new group and a new fictional "ghost."

REAL, RANDOM, OR RE-CREATION?

So what can be concluded from all this? No one knows for sure, but several schools of thought have developed regarding the matter. Some believe that Philip was a real ghost and that he had once been a living, breathing person. Perhaps he had a few of the characteristics of the fictional Philip and simply responded to the group's summons. Some who believe in the ghost theory say that it may have been a playful spirit (or a demonic one) that just pretended to be Philip as a prank.

A less-popular theory suggests that someone close to the group was aware of the background information as well as the times and places of the meetings. He or she might have planned an elaborate hoax to make it appear as though the ghost was real.

But it is also possible that after creating Philip, the Owen Group put forth enough energy, focus, and concentration to bring him to life, in a manner of speaking. Ghosts may well be products of our imaginations, existing only in our minds, but this study does prove one thing: When people put those minds together, anything is possible—even a visit from the Other Side.

UNIDENTIFIED SUBMERGED OBJECTS

Much like their flying brethren, unidentified submerged objects captivate and mystify. But instead of vanishing into the skies, USOs, such as the following, plunge underwater.

SIGHTING AT PUERTO RICO TRENCH

In 1963, while conducting exercises off the coast of Puerto Rico, U.S. Navy submarines encountered something extraordinary. The incident began when a sonar operator aboard an accompanying destroyer reported a strange occurrence. According to the seaman, one of the subs traveling with the armada broke free from the pack to chase a USO. This quarry would be unlike anything the submariners had ever pursued.

Underwater technology in the early 1960s was advancing rapidly. Still, vessels had their limitations. The U.S.S. *Nautilus*, though faster than any submarine that preceded it, was still limited to about 20 knots (23 miles per hour). The bathyscaphe *Trieste*, a deep-sea submersible, could exceed 30,000 feet in depth, but the descent took as long as five hours. Once there, the vessel could not be maneuvered side to side.

Knowing this, the submariners were stunned by what they witnessed. The USO was moving at 150 knots (170 miles per hour) and hitting depths greater than 20,000 feet! No underwater vehicles on Earth were capable of such fantastic numbers. Even today, modern nuclear subs have top speeds of about 25 knots (29 miles per hour) and can operate at around 800-plus feet below the surface.

Thirteen separate crafts witnessed the USO as it criss-crossed the Atlantic Ocean over a four-day period. At its deepest, the mystery vehicle reached 27,000 feet. To this day, there's been no earthly explanation offered for the occurrence.

USO WITH A BUS PASS

In 1964, London bus driver Bob Fall witnessed one of the strangest USO sightings. While transporting a full contingent of passengers, the driver and his fares reported seeing a silver, cigar-shape object dive into the nearby waters of the River Lea. The police attributed the phenomenon to a flight of ducks, despite the obvious incongruence. Severed telephone lines and a large gouge on the river's embankment suggested something far different.

SHAG HARBOUR INCIDENT

The fishing village of Shag Harbour lies on Canada's east coast. This unassuming hamlet is to USOs what Roswell, New Mexico, is to UFOs. Simply put, it played host to the most famous occurrence of a USO ever recorded.

On the evening of October 4, 1967, the Royal Canadian Mounted Police (RCMP) were barraged by reports of a UFO that had crashed into the bay at Shag Harbour. Laurie Wickens and four friends witnessed a large object (approximately 60 feet in diameter) falling into the water just after 11:00 p.m. Floating approximately 1,000 feet off the coast they could clearly detect a yellow light on top of the object.

The RCMP promptly contacted the Rescue Coordination Center in Halifax to ask if any aircraft were missing. None were. Shortly thereafter, the object sank into the depths of the water and disappeared from view.

When local fishing boats went to the USO crash site, they encountered yellow foam on the water's surface and detected an odd sulfuric smell. No survivors or bodies were ever found. The Royal Canadian Air Force officially labeled the occurrence a UFO, but because the object was last seen under water, such events are now described as USOs.

PASCAGOULA INCIDENT

On November 6, 1973, at approximately 8:00 p.m., a USO was sighted by at least nine fishermen anchored off the coast of Pascagoula, Mississippi. They witnessed an underwater object an estimated five feet in diameter that emitted a strange amber light.

First to spot the USO was Rayme Ryan. He repeatedly poked at the light-emitting object with an oar. Each time he made contact with the strange object, its light would dim and it would move a few feet away, then brighten once again. Fascinated by the ethereal quality of this submerged question mark, Ryan summoned the others. For the next half hour, the cat-and-mouse game played out in front of the fishermen until Ryan struck the object with a particularly forceful blow. With this action, the USO disappeared from view.

The anglers moved about a half-mile away and continued fishing. After about 30 minutes, they returned to their earlier location and were astounded to find that the USO had returned. At this point, they decided to alert the Coast Guard.

After interviewing the witnesses, investigators from the Naval Ship Research and Development Laboratory in Panama City, Florida, submitted their findings: At least nine persons had witnessed an undetermined light source whose characteristics and actions were inconsistent with those of known marine organisms or with an uncontrolled human-made object. Their final report was inconclusive, stating that the object could not be positively identified.

BACK FROM THE DEAD

Nothing is certain but death and taxes...yet sometimes that's not so true. History is riddled with strange tales of people who just weren't content staying dead.

❖ After a major automobile accident in 2007, Venezuelan Carlos Camejo was declared dead. The coroner had just begun the autopsy by cutting into Camejo's face when the man began to bleed. Immediately realizing that the crash victim was still alive, the doctor became even more stunned when Camejo regained consciousness as he was stitching up the incision. "I woke up because the pain was unbearable," Camejo told reporters after his ordeal.

❖ Ann Greene, a young servant in Oxford, England, was convicted of killing her illegitimate newborn child after the baby was stillborn in 1650. After she was hanged, Greene's body was cut down and transported to Oxford University where it was to be used for anatomy classes. As the lesson progressed, Greene began to moan and regained consciousness. The students helped revive her and treated her injuries. Eventually she was given a pardon, gained a level of celebrity, married, and had several children.

❖ In 1674, Marjorie Erskine died in Chirnside, Scotland, and was buried in a shallow grave by a sexton with less than honorable intentions. Erskine was sent to her eternal rest with some valuable jewelry the sexton was intent on adding to his own collection. After digging up her body, the sexton was trying to cut off her finger to steal her ring when, much to his surprise, she awoke.

❖ After being found unconscious and sprawled on the floor of her Albany, New York, apartment by paramedics in 1996, Mildred Clarke, 86, was pronounced dead by a coroner. About 90 minutes later an attendant noticed that the body bag containing Clarke was, in fact, moving. Clarke recovered but unfortunately only lived for another week, giving into the stress of age and heart failure.

❖ When 19th-century Cardinal Somaglia took ill and passed out, he was thought to be dead. Being a high-ranking church official, embalming was begun immediately so he could lie in state, as was customary. As a surgeon began the process by cutting into the cardinal's chest, he noticed that the man's heart was still beating. Somaglia awoke and pushed the knife away. However, the damage was done, and he died from the embalming process.

FIREBALL IN THE SKY

While playing football on the afternoon of September 12, 1952, a group of boys in Flatwoods, West Virginia, saw a large fireball fly over their heads. The object seemed to stop near the hillside property of Bailey Fisher. Some thought the object was a UFO, but others said it was just a meteor. They decided to investigate.

Darkness was falling as the boys made their way toward the hill, so they stopped at the home of Kathleen May to borrow a flashlight. Seeing how excited the boys were, May, her two sons, and their friend, Eugene Lemon, decided to join them. The group set off to find out exactly what had landed on the hill.

WALKING THROUGH THE DARKNESS

As they neared the top of the hill, the group smelled a strange odor that reminded them of burning metal. Continuing on, some members of the group thought they saw an object that resembled a spaceship. Shining their flashlights in front of them, the group was startled when something not of this world moved out from behind a nearby tree.

THE ENCOUNTER

The description of what is now known as the Flatwoods Monster is almost beyond belief. It stood around 12 feet tall and had a round, reddish face from which two large holes were visible. Looming up from behind the creature's head was a large pointed hood. The creature, which appeared to be made of a dark metal, had no arms or legs and seemed to float through the air. Looking back, the witnesses believe what they saw was a protective suit or perhaps a robot rather than a monster.

When a flashlight beam hit the creature, its "eyes" lit up and it began floating toward the group while making a strange hissing noise. The horrible stench was now overpowering and some in the group immediately felt nauseous. Because she was at the head of the group, Kathleen May had the best view of the monster. She later stated that as the creature was moving toward her, it squirted or dripped a strange fluid on her that resembled oil but had an unusual odor to it.

Terrified beyond belief, the group fled down the hillside and back to the May house, where they telephoned Sheriff Robert Carr, who responded with his deputy, Burnell Long. After talking with the group, they gathered some men and went to the Fisher property to investigate. But they only found a gummy residue and what appeared to be skid marks on the ground. There was no monster and no spaceship. However, the group did report that the heavy stench of what smelled like burning metal was still in the air.

THE AFTERMATH

A. Lee Stewart, a member of the of the search party and co- publisher of the *Braxton Democrat*, knew a good story when he saw one, so he sent the tale over the news wire, and almost immediately, people were asking Kathleen May for interviews. On September 19, 1952, May and Stewart discussed the Flatwoods Monster on the TV show *We the People*. For the show, an artist sketched the creature based on May's description, but he took some liberties, and the resulting sketch was so outrageous that people started saying the whole thing was a hoax.

Slowly, though, others came forward to admit that they too had seen a strange craft flying through the sky near Flatwoods on September 12. One witness described it as roughly the size of a single-car garage. He said that he lost sight of the craft when it appeared to land on a nearby hill.

Since that night in 1952, the Flatwoods Monster has never been seen again, leaving many people to wonder what exactly those people encountered. A monster? An alien from another world? Or perhaps nothing more than a giant owl? One thing is for sure: There were far too many witnesses to deny that they stumbled upon something strange that night.

PLAIN UNEXPLAINED

If a phenomenon can't be readily explained, does that make it any less true to those who witnessed it?

MOODUS NOISES

The Moodus Noises are thunderlike sounds that emanate from caves near East Haddam, Connecticut, where the Salmon and Moodus Rivers meet. The name itself is derived from the Native American word *machemoodus*, which means "place of noises." When European settlers filtered into the area in the late 1600s, the Wangunk tribe warned them about the odd, supernatural sounds. Whether or not anything otherworldly exists there is open to debate. In 1979, seismologists showed that the noises were always accompanied by small earthquakes (some measuring as low as magnitude 2 on the Richter scale) spread over a small area some 5,000 feet deep by 800 feet wide. But this doesn't explain the fact that no known fault line exists at Moodus. Nor does it describe how small tremors—producing 100 times less ground motion than is detectable by human beings—can generate big, bellowing booms. The mystery and the booms continue.

ROCK CONCERT

Visitors looking to entertain themselves at Pennsylvania's Ringing Rocks Park often show up toting hammers. Seems odd, but they're necessary for the proper tone. Ringing Rocks is a seven-acre boulder field that runs about ten feet deep. For reasons that are still unexplained, some of these rocks ring like bells when struck lightly by a hammer or other object. Because igneous diabase rocks don't usually do this, the boulder field has caused quite a stir through the years. In 1890, Dr. J. J. Ott held what may have been the world's first "rock concert" at the park. He assembled rocks of different pitches, enlisted the aid of a brass band for accompaniment, and went to town.

CRY ME A RED RIVER

Tales of "crying" statues have become almost commonplace. Sometimes they're revealed as hoaxes, but other times they can truly confound the senses. The Mother Mary statue that cries "tears of blood" at the Vietnamese Catholic Martyrs Church in Sacramento apparently began crying in November 2005 when parishioners discovered a dark reddish substance flowing from her left eye. A priest wiped it away only to see it miraculously reappear a moment later. News of the incident spread like...well, like news of a crying Mother Mary statue. Soon, hordes of the faithful made a pilgrimage to witness the miracle. Skeptics say that black paint used as eyeliner on the statue is the true culprit and that her "tears" are closer to this color than red. The faithful think the nonbelievers are blinded by anything but the light because the tears continually reappear even after the excess substance is wiped away.

THE WATSEKA WONDER

The story of the "Watseka Wonder," a phenomenon that occurred in a small town in Illinois in the late 1800s, still stands as one of the most authentic cases of spirit possession in history. It has been investigated, dissected, and ridiculed, but to this day, no clear explanation has ever been offered.

AN OTHERWORLDLY CONNECTION

Beginning on July 11, 1877, 13-year-old Watseka resident Lurancy Vennum started falling into strange trances that sometimes lasted for hours. During these trances, she claimed to speak with spirits and visit heaven. But when she awoke, she could not recall what had occurred during the spell.

LURANCY VENNUM

Doctors diagnosed Lurancy as mentally ill and recommended that she be sent to the state insane asylum. But in January 1878, a man named Asa Roff, who also lived in Watseka, visited the Vennums. He told them that his daughter Mary had displayed the same behavior as Lurancy nearly 13 years before, and he advised the family to keep Lurancy out of the asylum.

Roff explained that on July 5, 1865, his 19-year-old daughter Mary had died in the state insane asylum. In the beginning, strange voices filled her head. Then she fell into long trances where she spoke as though possessed by the spirits of the dead. She later developed an obsession with bloodletting, poking herself with pins, applying leeches to her body, and cutting herself with a razor. Finally, her parents took her to the asylum, where she died a short time later.

THE STRANGE CASE OF LURANCY VENNUM

At the time of Mary Roff's death, Lurancy Vennum was barely a year old. Born on April 16, 1864, Lurancy moved with her family to Watseka a few years after Mary Roff's death and knew nothing of the girl or her family. When Lurancy's attacks began in July 1877, her family had no idea that she was suffering from the same type of illness that Mary had.

On the morning of her first trance, Lurancy collapsed and fell into a deep sleep that lasted more than five hours. When she awoke, she seemed fine. But the spell returned again the next day, and this time, while Lurancy was unconscious, she spoke of seeing angels and walking in heaven. She told her family that she had talked to her brother, who had died three years before.

As rumors of Lurancy's affliction spread around town, Asa Roff realized how closely her symptoms mirrored those of his own daughter, and he was convinced that the illnesses were the same. Roff kept quiet, but when it was suggested that Lurancy be institutionalized, he knew he had to speak up.

When Roff contacted the Vennum family on January 31, 1878, they were skeptical, but they allowed him to bring Dr. E. Winchester Stevens to meet with Lurancy. Like Roff, Dr. Stevens was a spiritualist. They felt that Lurancy was not insane but was possessed by spirits of the dead.

When Dr. Stevens arrived, Lurancy began speaking in another voice, claiming that she was a woman named Katrina Hogan. A few moments later, her voice changed again, and she said that she was Willie Canning, a boy who had killed himself many years before. Willie spoke for more than an hour. Then, just as Dr. Stevens and Asa Roff prepared to leave, Lurancy threw her arms into the air and fell on the floor stiff as a board. After Dr. Stevens calmed her down, Lurancy claimed she was in heaven and that spirits, some good and some bad, were controlling her body. She said the good spirit who most wanted to control her was a young woman named Mary Roff..

THE RETURN OF MARY ROFF

After about a week of being possessed by the spirit of Mary Roff, Lurancy insisted on leaving the Vennum house, which was unfamiliar to her, and going "home" to the Roff house. When Mrs. Roff heard what was going on, she rushed over to the Vennum house with her daughter Minerva. As Lurancy watched the two women hurry up the sidewalk, she cried out, "There comes my ma and my sister Nervie!" "Nervie" had been Mary's pet name for her sister.

To those involved, it seemed evident that Mary's spirit had taken over Lurancy's body. She looked the same, but she knew nothing of the Vennum family or of her life as Lurancy. Instead, she had intimate knowledge of the Roffs and acted as though they were her family. Although Lurancy treated the Vennums politely, they were strangers to her.

On February 11, realizing that it was best for Lurancy, the Vennums allowed their daughter to go stay with the Roffs—although Lurancy told the Roffs that she would only be with them until "sometime in May."

On their way home, as the Roffs and Lurancy traveled past the house where they'd lived when Mary died, Lurancy wanted to know why they weren't stopping. The Roffs explained that they'd moved to a new home a few years back, which was something that Lurancy/Mary would not have known.

Within a short time, Lurancy began to exhibit signs that she knew more about the Roffs and their habits than she could have possibly known if she was only pretending to be Mary. She knew of incidents and experiences that were private and had taken place long before she was even born.

As promised, Lurancy stayed with the Roff family until early May. When it was time for Mary to leave Lurancy's body, she was deeply saddened, but she seemed to understand that it was time to go. On May 21, Lurancy returned to the Vennums. She showed no signs of her earlier illness, and her parents and the Roffs believed that she had been cured of her affliction by the possession of Mary's spirit.

Lurancy grew into a happy young woman and exhibited no ill effects from the possession. She married and had 13 children.

AN UNSOLVED MYSTERY

Although Lurancy had no memories of being possessed by Mary, she felt a closeness to the Roffs that she could never explain. She stayed in touch with the Roff family even after they moved away from Watseka in 1879. Each year, when they returned, Lurancy would allow Mary's spirit to possess her, and things were just as they were for a time in 1878.

THE GREENBRIER GHOST: TESTIMONY FROM THE OTHER SIDE

The strange tale of the Greenbrier Ghost stands out in the annals of ghost lore. Not only is it part of supernatural history, it is also part of the history of the U.S. judicial system. To this day, it is the only case in which a crime was solved and a murderer convicted based on the testimony of a ghost.

A DOOMED MARRIAGE

Little is known about her life, but it is believed that Zona Heaster was born in Greenbrier County, West Virginia, around 1873. In October 1896, she met Erasmus "Edward" Stribbling Trout Shue, a drifter who had recently moved to the area to work as a blacksmith. A short time later, the two were married, despite the animosity felt toward Shue by Zona's mother, Mary Jane Heaster, who had instantly disliked him.

Unfortunately, the marriage was short-lived. In January 1897, Zona's body was discovered at home by a young neighbor boy who had come to the house on an errand. After he found Zona lying on the floor at the bottom of the stairs, he ran to get the local doctor and coroner, Dr. George W. Knapp. By the time Dr. Knapp arrived, Shue had come home, found his wife, and carried her body upstairs where he laid her on the bed and dressed her in her best clothing—a high-necked, stiff-collared dress with a big scarf tied around her neck and a veil placed over her face.

While Dr. Knapp was examining Zona's body in an attempt to determine the cause of death, Shue allegedly stayed by his wife's side, cradling her head, sobbing, and clearly distressed over anyone touching her body. As a result, Knapp did not do a thorough examination. Although he did notice some bruising on Zona's neck, he initially listed her cause of death as "everlasting faint" and then as "childbirth." Whether or not Zona was pregnant is unknown, but Dr. Knapp had been treating her for some time prior to her death.

When Mary Jane Heaster was informed of her daughter's death, her face grew dark as she uttered: "The devil has killed her!" Zona's body was taken to her parents' home where it was displayed for the wake.

Those who came to pay their respects whispered about Shue's erratic behavior—one minute he'd be expressing intense grief and sadness, then displaying frenetic outbursts the next. He would not allow anyone to get close to the coffin, especially when he placed a pillow and a rolled-up cloth around his wife's head to help her "rest easier." Still, when Zona's body was moved to the cemetery, several people noted a strange looseness to her head. Not surprisingly, people started to talk.

GHOSTLY MESSAGES FROM THE OTHER SIDE

Mary Jane Heaster did not have to be convinced that Shue was acting suspiciously about Zona's death. She had always hated him and wished her daughter had never married him. She had a sneaking suspicion that something wasn't right, but she didn't know how to prove it.

After the funeral, as Heaster was folding the sheet from inside the coffin, she noticed that it had an unusual odor. When she placed it into the basin to wash it, the water turned red. Stranger still, the sheet turned pink and then the color in the water disappeared. Even after Heaster boiled the sheet, the stain remained. To her, the bizarre "bloodstains" were a sign that Zona had been murdered.

For the next four weeks, Heaster prayed fervently every night that Zona would come to her and explain the details of her death. Soon after, her prayers were answered. For four nights, Zona's spirit appeared at her mother's bedside, first as a bright light, but then the air in the room got cold and her apparition took form. She told her mother that Shue had been an abusive and cruel husband, and in a fit of rage, he'd attacked her because he thought she had not cooked any meat for supper. He'd broken her neck, and as evidence, Zona's ghost spun her head around until it was facing backward.

Heaster's suspicions were correct: Shue had killed Zona and she'd come back from beyond the grave to prove it.

OPENING THE GRAVE

After Zona's ghostly visit, Heaster tried to convince the local prosecutor, John Alfred Preston, to reopen the investigation into her daughter's death. She pleaded that an injustice was taking place and, as evidence, she told him about her encounters with Zona's spirit. Although it seems unlikely that he would reexamine the case because of the statement of a ghost, the investigation was, in fact, reopened. Preston agreed to question Dr. Knapp and a few others involved in the case. The local newspaper reported that a number of citizens were suspicious of Zona's death, and rumors were circulating throughout the community.

Dr. Knapp admitted to Preston that his examination of Zona's body was cursory at best, so it was agreed that an autopsy would be done to settle any lingering questions. They could find out how Zona really died, and, if he was innocent, ease the suspicions surrounding Shue.

The local newspaper reported that Shue "vigorously complained" about the exhumation and autopsy of his wife's body, but he was required to attend. A jury of five men gathered together in the chilly building to watch the autopsy along with officers of the court, Shue, and other witnesses.

The autopsy findings were rather damning to Shue. When the doctors concluded that Zona's neck had been broken, Shue's head dropped, and a dark expression crossed his face. "They cannot prove that I did it," he said quietly.

A March 9 report stated: "The discovery was made that the neck was broken and the windpipe mashed. On the throat were the marks of fingers indicating that she had been choken [sic]… The neck was dislocated between the first and second vertebrae. The ligaments were torn and ruptured. The windpipe had been crushed at a point in front of the neck."

Despite the fact that—aside from Zona's ghost—the evidence against Shue was circumstantial at best, he was arrested, indicted, and formally arraigned for murder. All the while, he maintained his innocence and entered a plea of "not guilty." He repeatedly told reporters that his guilt in the matter could not be proven.

While awaiting trial, details about Shue's unsavory past came to light. Zona was actually his third wife. In 1889, while he was in prison for horse theft, he was divorced from his first wife, Allie Estelline Cutlip, who claimed that Shue had frequently beaten her during their marriage. In fact, at one point, Shue allegedly beat Cutlip so severely that a group of men had to pull him off of her and throw him into an icy river.

In 1894, Shue married his second wife, Lucy Ann Tritt, who died just eight months later under mysterious circumstances. Shue left the area in the autumn of 1896 and moved to Greenbrier. When word got out that Shue was suspected of murdering Zona, stories started circulating about the circumstances behind Tritt's death, but no wrongdoing was ever proven.

Despite the fact that he was in jail, Shue seemed in good spirits. Remarking that he was done grieving for Zona, he revealed that it was his life's dream to have seven wives. Because Zona was only wife number three and he was still fairly young, he felt confident that he could achieve his goal.

TESTIMONY FROM A GHOST

When Shue's trial began in June 1897, numerous members of the community testified against him. Of course, Heaster's testimony was the highlight of the trial. She testified as both the mother of the victim and as the first person to notice the unusual circumstances of Zona's death. Preston wanted her to come across as sane and reliable, so he did not mention the spirit encounter, which would make Heaster look irrational and was also inadmissible as evidence. Zona's testimony obviously could not be cross-examined by the defense and, therefore, was hearsay under the law.

But unfortunately for Shue, his attorney did ask Heaster about her ghostly visit. Certainly, he was trying to destroy her credibility with the jury, characterizing her "visions" as the overactive imagination of a grieving mother. He was tenacious in trying to get her to admit that she was mistaken about what she'd seen, but Heaster zealously stuck to her story. When Shue's attorney realized that she was not going to budge from her story, he dismissed her.

But by then, the damage was done. Because the defense—not the prosecution—had brought up Zona's otherworldly testimony, the judge had a difficult time ordering the jury to ignore it. Clearly, most of the townspeople believed that Heaster really had been visited by her daughter's ghost. Shue testified in his own defense, but the jury quickly found him guilty. Ten of the jury members voted for Shue to be hanged, but because they could not reach a unanimous decision, he was sentenced to life in prison.

Shue didn't carry out his sentence for long—he died in March 1900 at the West Virginia State Penitentiary in Moundsville. Until her death in 1916, Heaster told her tale to anyone who would listen, never recanting her story of her daughter's ghostly visit.

It seems that after visiting her mother to offer details of her murder, Zona was finally able to rest in peace. Although her ghost was never seen again, she did leave a historical mark on Greenbrier County, where a roadside marker still commemorates the case today. It reads:

"Interred in nearby cemetery is Zona Heaster Shue. Her death in 1897 was presumed natural until her spirit appeared to her mother to describe how she was killed by her husband Edward. Autopsy on the exhumed body verified the apparition's account. Edward, found guilty of murder, was sentenced to the state prison. Only known case in which testimony from ghost helped convict a murderer."

WEIRD WEATHER

We've all heard that neither rain, snow, sleet nor hail, will stop our determined mail carriers, but how about a few rounds of ball lightning or tiny frogs dropping from the sky? Apparently, Mother Nature has a sense of humor. Here are some of the weirdest weather phenomena encountered on Planet Earth.

GOODNESS, GRACIOUS, GREAT BALLS OF LIGHTNING!

Perhaps it was ball lightning, an unexplained spherical mass of electrical energy, that Jerry

Lee Lewis was singing about in the popular tune "Great Balls of Fire." In 1976, the strange phenomenon supposedly attacked a woman in the UK as she ironed during an electrical storm. A ball of lightning emerged from her iron, spun around the room, then threw her across the room, ripping off half her clothes in the process. In 1962, a Long Island couple was astounded to see a fiery, basketball-size orb roll into their living room through an open window. The fireball passed between the pair, continued through the room, and disappeared down an adjacent hallway. Exactly how lightning or any other electrical anomaly can form itself into a ball and zigzag at different speeds is not well understood.

OTHERWORLDLY LIGHTS: ST. ELMO'S FIRE

A weird haze of light glimmering around a church steeple during a storm, a rosy halo over someone's head, or a ghostly light swirling around the mast of a wave-tossed ship—these are all possible manifestations of the strange, bluish-white light known as St. Elmo's Fire, which may be a signal that a lightning strike to the glowing area is imminent. The light is a visible, electric discharge produced by heavy storms. It was named after St. Erasmus, aka St. Elmo, the patron saint of sailors.

WHEN THE MOON GETS THE BLUES

Everyone understands that the phrase "once in a blue moon" refers to a very unusual occurrence, since blue moons are rare. But a blue moon is not actually blue. In fact, a blue moon is determined by the calendar, not by its color. Typically, there is one full moon per month, but occasionally, a second full moon will sneak into a monthly cycle. When this happens, the second full moon is referred to as a "blue moon," which happens every two to three years. But at times, the moon has been known to appear blue, or even green, often after a volcanic eruption leaves tiny ash and dust particles in the earth's atmosphere.

GREEN FLASH: THE SUN GOES GREEN

The term *green flash* may sound like a comic book superhero, but it is actually a strange flash of green light that appears just before the setting sun sinks into the horizon. Some have suggested that rare fluctuations in solar winds may be responsible for green glows and flashes that sometimes appear in the atmosphere just before sunset. Some believe it's just a mirage. But others contend that a green flash occurs when layers of the earth's atmosphere act like a prism. Whatever causes the emerald hue, seeing a flash of green light along the horizon can be an eerie and unsettling experience.

DOUBLE THE RAINBOWS, DOUBLE THE GOLD?

Rainbow stories abound; ancient Irish lore promises a pot of leprechaun's gold at the end of a rainbow, and biblical tradition says God set a rainbow in the sky as a promise to Noah that Earth would never again be destroyed by water. Rainbows are formed when sunlight passes through water droplets, usually at the end of a rainstorm, and the droplets separate the light like tiny prisms into a spectrum from red to violet. A secondary rainbow, set outside the first one and in the reverse order of colors, is formed by a second set of light refractions to create the spectacular double rainbow. Conditions have to be just right to see the double rainbow because the secondary arch of colors is much paler than the primary rainbow and is not always visible.

LAVA LAMPS IN THE SKY: AURORA BOREALIS

Like a neon sign loosened from its tubing, the aurora borealis sends multicolored arches, bands, and streams of luminous beauty throughout the northern skies whenever solar flares are at their height. This occurs when electrons ejected from the sun's surface hit Earth's atmospheric particles and charge them until they glow. The electrons are attracted to Earth's magnetic poles, which is why they are seen mainly in the far northern or southern latitudes. In the southern hemisphere, they are called aurora australis. Aurora Polaris refers to the lights of either pole.

IT'S RAINING FROGS!

Startling as the thought of being pelted from above by buckets of hapless amphibians may be, reports of the sky raining frogs have occurred for so long that the problem was even addressed in the 1st century AD, when a Roman scholar, Pliny the Elder, theorized that frog "seeds" were already present in the soil. But in 2005, residents of Serbia were shocked when masses of teensy toads tumbled out of a dark cloud that suddenly appeared in the clear blue sky. Scientific American reported a frog fall over Kansas City, Missouri, in July 1873, in numbers so thick they "darkened the air." And in Birmingham, England, the froglets that reportedly dropped from the heavens on June 30, 1892, were not green but a milky white. In 1987, pink frogs fell in Gloucestershire, England. No one knows for certain why this happens, but one theory is that the small animals—fish, birds, and lizards are also common—are carried from other locations by tornadoes or waterspouts.

SPOUTING OFF

Ancient people feared waterspouts and understandably

so. Waterspouts are actually tornadoes that form over a body of water, whirling at speeds as fast as 190 miles per hour. Waterspouts start with parent clouds that pull air near the surface into a vortex at an increasing rate, until water is pulled up toward the cloud. One of the world's top waterspout hot spots is the Florida Keys, which may see as many as 500 per year. They can also occur in relatively calm areas such as Lake Tahoe, on the California–Nevada border. There, a Native American legend said that waterspouts, which they called "waterbabies," appeared at the passing of great chiefs to take them to heaven.

MIRAGES: OPTICAL CONFUSION

Mirages have been blamed for everything from imaginary waterholes in deserts to sightings of the Loch Ness Monster. They come in two forms: hallucinations or environmental illusions based on tricks of light, shadow, and atmosphere. In April 1977, residents of Grand Haven, Michigan, were able to plainly see the shimmering lights of Milwaukee, Wisconsin, some 75 miles across Lake Michigan. The sighting was confirmed by the flashing pattern of Milwaukee's red harbor beacon. Another rare type of water mirage is the *fata morgana*, which produces a double image that makes mundane objects look gigantic and may account for some reports of sea monsters.

COBWEBS FROM HEAVEN?

On their 40-year desert tour with Moses, the Israelites were blessed with a strange substance called manna that fell from the sky. People in other places have also witnessed falls of unknown material, often resembling cobwebs. In October 1881, great quantities of weblike material fell around the cities of Milwaukee, Green Bay, and Sheboygan, Wisconsin. Newspapers speculated that the strong, white strands had come from "gossamer spiders" due to their lightness. The same thing allegedly happened in 1898 in Montgomery, Alabama. Not all falls of unknown material have been so pleasant—a yellowish, smelly substance fell on Kourianof, Russia, in 1832, and something similar was reported in Ireland around 1695.

CREEPY COINCIDENCES

From a prophetic book written decades before a tragic event took place to a man struck repeatedly by lightning, life's great coincidences are often truly mind-boggling.

THE NUMBERS DON'T LIE

The terror attacks of September 11, 2001, brought with them much speculation. Was this heinous act perpetrated by a group of rogue extremists or part of a larger conspiracy? Did everything happen precisely as reported, or was the public being misled? While these questions and others were being pondered, a curious and underreported event took place.

On September 11, 2002, the one-year anniversary of the attacks, the New York State Lottery conducted one of two standard daily drawings. In the three-number contest, the balls drawn were 9–1–1. Statisticians point out that this isn't particularly astounding, given the less than astronomical odds in a three-ball draw. Even so, that's one creepy coincidence.

WOMB FOR ONE MORE

As if one womb were no longer good enough to get the job done, Hannah Kersey of Great Britain was born with two. Then, in 2006, to confound the medical world even more, the 23-year-old woman gave birth to triplets—

identical twins Ruby and Tilly were delivered from one of Kersey's wombs, while baby Gracie was extracted from the other. All three girls came into the world seven weeks premature via cesarean section and were quite healthy upon arrival. For the record, there have been about 70 known pregnancies in separate wombs in the past 100 years, but the case of triplets is the first of its kind and doctors estimate the likelihood is about one in 25 million.

HE'S AWL THAT

Most people recognize the name Louis Braille, the world-renowned inventor of the Braille system of reading and writing for the blind. But what many people don't know is how Braille himself became blind and how it led to his invention.

When he was only three years old, Braille accidentally poked himself in the eye with a stitching awl owned by his father, a saddle maker. At first his injury didn't seem serious, but when an autoimmune disease known as sympathetic ophthalmia set in, he went blind in both eyes.

Over the years, Braille adapted well to his disability. Then, in 1824, at age 15, he invented a system of raised dots that enabled the blind to read and write through use of their fingertips. To form each dot on a page, Braille employed a common hand tool found at most saddle maker's shops—a stitching awl, the same tool that had injured him as a child.

LOTSA LUCK

Evelyn Adams had a couple of bucks and a dream. In 1985, she purchased a New Jersey lottery ticket and crossed her fingers. When the winning numbers were called, she realized she had hit the jackpot. The following year, Adams amazingly hit the jackpot once more. Her combined take for both wins totaled a cool $5.4 million. It was enough money to easily live out her days in comfort. But it wasn't to be. Due to Adams's innate generosity and love of gambling, she eventually went broke. Today, she lives in a trailer and laments the past: "I wish I had the chance to do it all over again. I'd be much smarter about it now."

THINK OF LAURA

On a whim, ten-year-old Laura Buxton of Burton, Staffordshire, England, jotted her name and address on a luggage label in 2001. She then attached it to a helium balloon and released it into the sky. Supported by air currents for 140 miles, the balloon eventually touched down in a garden in Pewsey, Wiltshire, England. Bizarrely, another ten-year-old girl named Laura Buxton read the note, got in touch with its sender, and the girls became fast friends. In addition to their identical names and ages, each child had fair hair and owned a black Labrador retriever, a guinea pig, and a rabbit.

ATTRACTIVE GENT

Do some people attract lightning the way a movie star attracts fans? In the case of Major Walter Summerford, an officer in the British Army, the evidence nods toward the affirmative. In 1918, Summerford received his first jolt when he was knocked from his horse by a flash of lightning. Injuries to his lower body forced him to retire from the military, so he moved to Vancouver, British Columbia.

In 1924, Summerford spent a day fishing beside a river. Suddenly, a bolt of lightning struck the tree he was sitting beneath, and he was zapped again. But by 1926, Summerford had recovered from his injuries to the degree that he was able to take walks. He continued with this therapy until one tragic summer's day in 1930 when, unbelievably, lightning found him yet again. This time it paralyzed him for good. He died two years after the incident.

The story should end there, but it doesn't. In 1936, a lightning bolt took aim at a cemetery and unleashed its 100,000-volt charge. Luckily, no living soul was nearby at the time, and the bolt passed its energy harmlessly into the ground, as do the vast majority of lightning strikes. Still, before hitting the ground, the lightning bolt injected its fearsome energy into Major Summerford's headstone.

FOUR'S A CROWD

In 1838, Edgar Allan Poe, famous author of the macabre, penned a novel entitled *The Narrative of Arthur Gordon Pym of Nantucket*. His fictitious account centers around four survivors of a shipwreck who find themselves adrift in an open lifeboat. After many days of hunger and torment, they decide the only way for any of them to survive is if one is sacrificed for food. They draw straws, and cabin boy Richard Parker comes up short. He is subsequently killed, and the three remaining seamen partake of his flesh.

In 1884, some 46 years after the tale was first told, the yacht *Mignonette* broke apart during a hurricane in the South Atlantic. Its four survivors drifted in a lifeboat for 19 days before turning desperate from hunger and thirst. One sailor, a cabin boy, became delirious after guzzling copious quantities of seawater. Upon seeing this, the other three determined that the man was at death's door and decided to kill him. They then devoured his remains. His name: Richard Parker.

DOWNED DAMSELS

Mary Ashford was born in 1797, and Barbara Forrest in 1954, yet circumstances surrounding their eventual murders are eerily similar. On May 27, 1817, Ashford was raped and killed in Erdington, England. On May 27, 1974, Forrest was also raped and murdered in Erdington, just 400 yards away from the site of Ashford's murder. The day preceding both of the murders was Whit Monday, a floating religious holiday on the Christian calendar celebrated mostly in Europe. The murders occurred at approximately the same time of day, and attempts had been made to conceal both bodies.

That's not all. Each woman had visited a friend on the night before Whit Monday, changed into a new dress during the evening, and attended a dance. Curiously, suspects in both cases shared the surname "Thornton." Both were subsequently tried and acquitted of murder. Paintings and photos show that the two women also shared very similar facial features.

NAUGHTY BUT NICE

Whenever Brownsville, Texas, waitress Melina Salazar saw cantankerous customer Walter "Buck" Swords walking into her café, she felt an urge to walk out. Nevertheless, Salazar persevered through a fusillade of demands and curses heaped upon her by her most demanding, albeit loyal, customer.

When 89-year-old Swords passed away, no one was more shocked than Salazar to learn that he'd bequeathed her $50,000 and his car. Describing Swords as, "kind of mean," the waitress told a television news crew, "I still can't believe it."

THE MYSTERIOUS ORB

If Texas were a dartboard, the city of Brownwood would be at the center of the bull's-eye. Maybe that's how aliens saw it, too.

Brownwood is a peaceful little city with about 20,000 residents and a popular train museum. A frontier town at one time, it became the trade center of Texas when the railroad arrived in 1885. Since then, the city has maintained a peaceful lifestyle. Even the massive tornado that struck Brownwood in 1976 left no fatalities. The place just has that "small town" kind of feeling.

AN INVADER FROM THE SKY

In July 2002, however, the city's peace was broken. Brownwood made international headlines when a strange metal orb fell from space, landed in the Colorado River, and washed up just south of town. The orb looked like a battered metal soccer ball—it was about a foot across, and it weighed just under ten pounds. Experts described it as a titanium sphere. When it was x-rayed, it revealed a second, inner sphere with tubes and wires wrapped inside.

That's all that anybody knows (or claims to know). No one is sure what the object is, and no one has claimed responsibility for it. The leading theory is that it's a cryogenic tank from some kind of spacecraft from Earth, used to store a small amount of liquid hydrogen or helium for cooling purposes. Others have speculated that it's a bomb, a spying device, or even a weapon used to combat UFOs.

IT'S NOT ALONE

The Brownwood sphere isn't unique. A similar object

landed in Kingsbury, Texas, in 1997, and was quickly confiscated by the Air Force for "tests and analysis." So far, no further announcements have been made.

Of course, the Air Force probably has a lot to keep it busy. About 200 UFOs are reported each month, and Texas is among the top three states where UFOs are seen. But until anything is known for sure, those in Texas at night should keep an eye on the skies.

THE GREAT TEXAS AIRSHIP MYSTERY

Roswell, New Mexico, may be the most famous potential UFO crash site, but did Texas experience a similar event in the 19th century?

One sunny April morning in 1897, a UFO crashed in Aurora, Texas.

Six years before the Wright Brothers' first flight and 50 years before Roswell, a huge, cigar-shape UFO was seen in the skies. It was first noted on November 17, 1896, about a thousand feet above rooftops in Sacramento, California. From there, the spaceship traveled to San Francisco, where it was seen by hundreds of people.

A NATIONAL TOUR

Next, the craft crossed the United States, where it was observed by thousands. Near Omaha, Nebraska, a farmer reported the ship on the ground, making repairs. When it returned to the skies, it headed toward Chicago, where it was photographed on April 11, 1897, the first UFO photo on record. On April 15, near Kalamazoo, Michigan, residents reported loud noises "like that of heavy ordnance" coming from the spaceship.

Two days later, the UFO attempted a landing in Aurora, Texas, which should have been a good place. The town was almost deserted, and its broad, empty fields could have been an ideal landing strip.

NO SMOOTH SAILING

However, at about 6:00 a.m. on April 17, the huge, cigar-shape airship "sailed over the public square and, when it reached the north part of town, collided with the tower of Judge Proctor's windmill and went to pieces with a terrific explosion, scattering debris over several acres of ground, wrecking the windmill and water tank and destroying the judge's flower garden."

That's how Aurora resident and cotton buyer S. E. Haydon described the events for *The Dallas Morning News*. The remains of the ship seemed to be strips and shards of a silver-colored metal. Just one body was recovered. The newspaper reported, "while his remains are badly disfigured, enough of the original has been picked up to show that he was not an inhabitant of this world."

On April 18, reportedly, that body was given a good, Christian burial in the Aurora cemetery, where it may remain to this day. A 1973 effort to exhume the body and examine it was successfully blocked by the Aurora Cemetery Association.

A FIRSTHAND ACCOUNT

Although many people have claimed the Aurora incident was a hoax, an elderly woman was interviewed in 1973 and clearly recalled the crash from her childhood. She said that her parents wouldn't let her near the debris from the spacecraft, in case it contained something dangerous. However, she described the alien as "a small man."

Aurora continues to attract people interested in UFOs. They wonder why modern Aurora appears to be laid out like a military base. Nearby, Fort Worth seems to be home to the U.S. government's experts in alien technology. Immediately after the Roswell UFO crash in 1947, debris from that spaceship was sent to Fort Worth for analysis.

IS THERE ANY TRACE LEFT?

The Aurora Encounter, a 1986 movie, documents the events that began when people saw the spacecraft attempt a landing at Judge Proctor's farm. Today, the Oates gas station marks the area where the UFO crashed. Metal debris was collected from the site in the 1970s and studied by North Texas State University. That study called one fragment "most intriguing": It appeared to be iron but wasn't magnetic; it was shiny and malleable rather than brittle, as iron should be.

As recently as 2008, UFOs have appeared in the north central Texas skies. In Stephenville, a freight company owner and pilot described a low-flying object in the sky, "a mile long and half a mile wide." Others who saw the ship several times during January 2008 said that its lights changed configuration, so it wasn't an airplane. The government declined to comment.

Today, a plaque at the Aurora cemetery mentions the spaceship, but the alien's tombstone—which, if it actually existed, is said to have featured a carved image of a spaceship—was stolen many years ago.

E. T. PHONE...CANADA?

Do extraterrestrials prefer Canada? The nation ranks first in UFO sightings per capita, with a record high of 1,004 reported in 2008 and 10 percent of Canadians claiming to have encountered one.

WHAT'S THAT?

Though recorded instances of UFO sightings on Canadian soil date back to the 1950s, extraterrestrial encounters emerged most prominently on the global radar in 1967 with two startling occurrences. The first happened when a quartz prospector near a mine at Falcon Lake in Manitoba was allegedly burned by a UFO.

The second followed in October of that year at Shag Harbour, Nova Scotia, when several witnesses—including residents, the Royal Canadian Mounted Police, and an Air Canada pilot—reported strange lights hovering above the water and then submerging. A search of the site revealed only odd yellow foam, suggesting something had indeed gone underwater, but whether it was a UFO remains a mystery.

A GROWING PHENOMENON

Since then, the number of sightings in Canada has increased nearly every year. Most take place in sparsely populated regions—the rationale being that "urban glow" obscures the lights of spaceships and that country folk spend more time outdoors and thus have better opportunities to glimpse UFOs. It may also be that rural areas are simply more conducive to extraterrestrial activity. (We've heard of crop circles, but parking garage circles? Not so much.)

Most sightings reported are of the "strange light" and "weird flying vessel" variety, and indeed most have rather banal explanations (stars, airplanes, towers). Still, each year between 1 and 10 percent of sightings remain a mystery.

JOHN LENNON SEES A UFO

LUCY IN THE SKY WITH WARP DRIVE.

In May 1974, former Beatle John Lennon and his assistant/mistress May Pang returned to New York City after almost a year's stay in Los Angeles, a period to which Lennon would later refer as his "Lost Weekend." The pair moved into Penthouse Tower B at 434 East 52nd Street. As Lennon watched television on a hot summer night, he noticed flashing lights reflected in the glass of an open door that led onto a patio. At first dismissing it as a neon sign, Lennon suddenly realized that since the apartment was on the roof, the glass couldn't be reflecting light from the street. So—sans clothing—he ventured onto the terrace to investigate. What he witnessed has never been satisfactorily explained.

SPEECHLESS

As Pang recollected, Lennon excitedly called for her to come outside. Pang did so. "I looked up and stopped mid-sentence," she said later. "I couldn't even speak because I saw this thing up there...it was silvery, and it was flying very slowly. There was a white light shining around the rim and a red light on the top...[it] was silent. We started to watch it drift down, tilt slightly, and it was flying below rooftops. It was the most amazing sight." She quickly ran back into the apartment, grabbed her camera, and returned to the patio, clicking away.

Lennon friend and rock photography legend Bob Gruen picked up the story: "In those days, you didn't have answering machines, but a service [staffed by people], and I had received a call from 'Dr. Winston.'" (Lennon's original middle name was Winston, and he often used the alias "Dr. Winston O'Boogie.") When Gruen returned the call, Lennon explained his incredible sighting and insisted that the photographer come round to pick up and develop the film personally. "He was serious," Gruen said. "He wouldn't call me in the middle of the night to joke around." Gruen noted that although Lennon had been known to partake in mind-altering substances in the past, during this period he was totally straight. So was Pang, a nondrinker who never took drugs and whom Gruen characterized as "a clear-headed young woman."

The film in Pang's camera was a unique type supplied by Gruen, "four times as fast as the highest speed then [commercially] available." Gruen had been using this specialty film, usually employed for military reconnaissance, in low-light situations such as recording studios. The same roll already had photos of Lennon and former bandmate Ringo Starr, taken by Pang in Las Vegas during a recording session.

Gruen asked Lennon if he'd reported his sighting to the authorities. "Yeah, like I'm going to call the police and say I'm John Lennon and I've seen a flying saucer," the musician scoffed. Gruen picked up the couple's phone and contacted the police, *The Daily News*, and the *New York Times*. The photographer claims that the cops and the *News* admitted that they'd heard similar reports, while the *Times* just hung up on him.

IT WOULD HAVE BEEN THE ULTIMATE TRIP

Gruen's most amusing recollection of Lennon, who had been hollering "UFO!" and "Take me with you!" was that none of his NYC neighbors either saw or heard the naked, ex-Beatle screaming from his penthouse terrace. And disappointingly, no one who might have piloted the craft responded to Lennon's pleas.

Gruen took the exposed film home to process, "sandwiching" it between two rolls of his own. Gruen's negatives came out perfectly, but the film Pang shot was "like a clear plastic strip," Gruen says. "We were all baffled... that it was completely blank."

Lennon remained convinced of what he'd seen. In several shots from a subsequent photo session with Gruen that produced the iconic shot of the musician wearing a New York City T-shirt (a gift from the photographer), John points to where he'd spotted the craft. And on his *Walls and Bridges* album, Lennon wrote in the liner notes: "On the 23rd Aug. 1974 at 9 o'clock I saw a U.F.O.—J.L."

Who's to say he and May Pang didn't? Certainly not Gruen, who still declares—more than 35 years after the fact—"I believed them."

And so the mystery remains.

EZEKIEL'S WHEEL: WHAT IN THE WORLD? VISION? UFO?

This scriptural passage is responsible for some of the most interesting speculation in the Bible's history. What was Ezekiel seeing?

SCRIPTURAL DESCRIPTION

Going to the source (Ezekiel 1), first the prophet describes some extremely strange living creatures in a fiery cloud: humanoids with four faces (human, eagle, ox, lion), four wings, bronze bodies, surrounding something like fiery coals. Then (verses 15–21):

As I looked at the living creatures, I saw a wheel on the earth beside the living creatures, one for each of the four of them. As for the appearance of the wheels and their construction: their appearance was like the gleaming of beryl; and the four had the same form, their construction being something like a wheel within a wheel. When they moved, they moved in any of the four directions without veering as they moved. Their rims were tall and awesome, for the rims of all four were full of eyes all around. When the living creatures moved, the wheels moved beside them; and when the living creatures rose from the earth, the wheels rose. Wherever the spirit would go, they went, and the wheels rose along with them; for the spirit of the living creatures was in the wheels. When they moved, the others moved; when they stopped, the others stopped; and when they rose from the earth, the wheels rose along with them; for the spirit of the living creatures was in the wheels.

Any lesser person than an Old Testament prophet of God might take a few aspirin and swear off "drink" for life.

OTHERWORLDLY INTERPRETATIONS

Plenty of artists have tried to depict Ezekiel's wheel. Most efforts look like gyroscopes: two shining circles intersecting. Picture a globe with a steel-blue ring around the equator. Imagine another metallic ring at a right angle to the first, passing through the North and South Poles. Subtract the globe. Could this be an ancient spaceship? All we have going for us is our science-fiction ideas of alien spacecraft. Some very educated minds suggest that Ezekiel is indeed describing a credible alien spaceship. We can't prove either way.

One book that fueled much of the speculation was *Chariots of the Gods?* (1968, Erich von Däniken). Von Däniken's thesis—that many ancient writings about gods, including the Bible, refer to contact with aliens—is unacceptable to most believers. Therefore, his thesis hasn't gained lasting traction with Jews and Christians. Nevertheless, some suspect that, with regard to Ezekiel 1, von Däniken had a grain of the truth.

NON-SCIENCE-FICTION VIEWS

Since we can only speculate, let's do so: The simplest explanation might be an angelic vision of the Lord's might. Ezekiel seems to have thought so (see Ezekiel 10) when he reflected on the matter. Perhaps the four forms represent archangels. They could also represent the four Gospels, identifying Matthew with the lion, Mark with the ox, Luke with the man, and John with the eagle.

Considering that Ezekiel's vision came from God, one might consider the "rims...full of eyes all around" to mean that God sees everything in all directions. One supposes that Ezekiel, as a believer, wouldn't normally need a reminder of this—but perhaps the Lord felt he did, or he wanted to dramatize it. That veers into trying to guess God's motives, which is problematic for the human mind.

One mainstream Jewish view, according to rabbinic wisdom and analysis, is that Ezekiel saw a heavenly chariot/throne bearing Hashem (God). It represented a vision of the Lord, a symbol of his ultimate generosity in showing his glory to his people. Given the location—near Babylon (modern Iraq)—it could foretell the equipment the region's main product (oil) would fuel someday.

We don't know. We can, however, compare the theories of the learned and determine for ourselves with the minds God gave us.

PREDICTIONS, PREMONITIONS, AND PRECOGNITION

Some believe strongly in precognition, while others aren't so sure, but when it arrives it's mighty hard to explain. Here are some freakishly accurate premonitions that might just stand your hair on end.

CAYCE AT BAT

Edgar Cayce (1877-1945) is to prophets what ballplayer Derek Jeter is to the Yankees. As one of the most reliable seers, Cayce, like Jeter, got the job done much of the time. Fittingly referred to as The Sleeping Prophet, Cayce would enter a trancelike state before issuing his readings. While in this state, Cayce predicted the stock market crash of 1929 six months before it occurred; the beginning of both world wars; the death of President Franklin D. Roosevelt; and the assassination of President John F. Kennedy.

HOY FORESEES TRAGEDY

On April 19, 1995, during a live radio program in Fayetteville, N.C., clairvoyant Tana Hoy hit prophecy pay dirt when he told the interviewer that there would be a deadly terrorist attack on a building in an American city beginning with the letter *O*. He added that the tragedy would occur before the first of May. Just 90 minutes later, the Alfred P. Murrah Federal Building in Oklahoma City was blown up by Timothy McVeigh and other radicals in what was, up to that point, the worst terrorist attack on U.S. soil.

TWAIN TO SEE

Writer Mark Twain (Samuel Clemons) eerily predicted the deaths of both his brother and himself. In a prophetic dream, Twain saw his brother laid out in a coffin resting between two folding chairs in his sister's parlor. A few weeks after the unsettling vision, Twain's brother was killed in a boating accident. When Twain entered his sister's living room to pay his last respects to his sibling, his eyes were confronted  by a startling sight. Before him lay his brother in a coffin stretched across two folding chairs—precisely as he had envisioned the scene during his dream.

Twain was born in 1835, the year that Halley's Comet was visible. He believed that his life force would be extinguished when Halley's Comet came back for its encore. In 1910, Halley's Comet came back into view. And Mark Twain exited the mortal world. Coincidence?

ROCKIN' OUT IN THE AFTERLIFE

Twain certainly wasn't alone in predicting his own death. Reports that President Abraham Lincoln witnessed his own assassination in a dream have long made the rounds, but the premonition lacks substantiation and is considered dubious.

Harder to discount is the vision that bassist Mikey Welsh had on September 26, 2011. A former member of the rock band Weezer, Welsh logged onto his Twitter account and issued the following statement: "Dreamt I died in Chicago next weekend (heart attack in my sleep). Need to write my will today."

Then, before signing off Welsh added this: "Correction—the weekend after next."

Two weeks later Welsh travelled to Chicago for Riot-fest—an annual rock music festival that was featuring his former band. Unfortunately, he never made it to the show. Staff at the Raffaello Hotel found Welsh's body in his room on October, 8, 2011, one day before the scheduled concert.

His death came as the result of an apparent drug overdose that in turn led to a heart attack. The time of his passing meshed precisely with his prediction.

PSYCHIC DETECTIVES

When the corpse just can't be found, the murderer remains unknown, and the weapon has been stashed in some secret corner, criminal investigations hit a stalemate and law enforcement agencies may tap their secret weapons—individuals who find things through some unconventional and unexplained methods.

"READING" THE RIPPER: ROBERT JAMES LEES

When the psychotic murderer known as Jack the Ripper terrorized London in the 1880s, the detectives of Scotland Yard consulted a psychic named Robert James Lees who said he had glimpsed the killer's face in several visions. Lees also claimed he had correctly forecasted at least three of the well-publicized murders of women. The Ripper wrote a sarcastic note to detectives stating that they would still never catch him. Indeed, the killer proved right in this prediction.

FEELING THEIR VIBES: FLORENCE STERNFELS

As a psychometrist—a psychic who gathers impressions by handling material objects—Florence Sternfels was successful enough to charge a dollar for readings in Edgewater, New Jersey, in the early 20th century. Born in 1891, Sternfels believed that her gift was a natural ability rather than a supernatural one, so she never billed police for her help in solving crimes. Some of her best "hits" included preventing a man from blowing up an army base with dynamite, finding two missing boys alive in Philadelphia, and leading police to the body of a murdered young woman. She worked with police as far away as Europe to solve tough cases but lived quietly in New Jersey until her death in 1965.

THE DUTCH GROCER'S GIFT: GERARD CROISET

Born in the Netherlands in 1909, Gerard Croiset nurtured a growing psychic ability from age six. In 1935, he joined a Spiritualist group, began to hone his talents, and within two years had set up shop as a psychic and healer. After a touring lecturer discovered his abilities in

1945, Croiset began assisting law enforcement agencies around the world, traveling as far as Japan and Australia. He specialized in finding missing children but also helped authorities locate lost papers and artifacts. At the same time, Croiset ran a popular clinic for psychic healing that treated both humans and animals. His son, Gerard Croiset, Jr., was also a professional psychic and parapsychologist.

ACCIDENTAL PSYCHIC: PETER HURKOS

As one of the most famous psychic detectives of the 20th century, Peter Hurkos did his best work by picking up vibes from victims' clothing. Born in the Netherlands in 1911, Hurkos lived an ordinary life as a house painter until a fall required him to undergo brain surgery at age 30. The operation seemed to trigger his latent psychic powers, and he was almost immediately able to mentally retrieve information about people and "read" the history of objects by handling them.

Hurkos assisted in the Boston Strangler investigation in the early 1960s, and in 1969, he was brought in to help solve the grisly murders executed by Charles Manson. He gave police many accurate details including the name Charlie, a description of Manson, and that the murders were ritual slayings.

THE TV SCREEN MIND OF DOROTHY ALLISON

New Jersey housewife Dorothy Allison broke into the world of clairvoyant crime solving when she dreamed about a missing local boy as if seeing it on television. In her dream, the five-year-old boy was stuck in some kind of pipe. When she called police, she also described the child's clothing, including the odd fact that he was wearing his shoes on the opposite feet. When Allison underwent hypnosis to learn more details, she added that the boy's